FUGAL ANSWER

FUGAL ANSWER

CHARLES NALDEN

1970

AUCKLAND UNIVERSITY PRESS
OXFORD UNIVERSITY PRESS

© Charles Nalden 1969

PRINTED IN GREAT BRITAIN
LOWE AND BRYDONE (PRINTERS) LTD., LONDON

To my Wife

The various Sentiments and Events that can be expressed in Musick introduce every moment a Novelty which cannot be reduced to fixed rules.

Jean Philippe Rameau
(*Traité de l'harmonie*)

FOREWORD

The title of this study takes the reader directly to a crossroad in music history—a crossroad barricaded for generations by constricting and misleading rules. The fascination of the phenomenon of fugal answer is that it embodies a basic problem of Western musical thought: the conflict and reconciliation of melody and harmony.

The conflict has been wrongly extended to a conflict of doctrine and reality which the author has outlined in the present study, and it is interesting that the opposing spokesmen quoted in the introduction are nineteenth century theorists and twentieth century historians. The reconciliation has been a true challenge to theory. Theorists have failed where they dealt with the questions of fugal technique as isolated issues; they have succeeded where they were guided by a wide view and by the realization that fugal theory itself must bring about a reconciliation of theory and history.

It is this challenge that the author has taken up, and his work is a doubly welcome contribution to the literature on fugue at a time when the academic significance of fugal study has grown rather than diminished, reminding the student that music is indeed a liberal art.

ALFRED MANN

ACKNOWLEDGEMENTS

I should like to thank Dr Alfred Mann of Rutgers University for reading the typescript, for his patient and detailed replies to my many queries, and for his kindly encouragement. My thanks are also due to Mr Michael Anderson, Librarian of the Reid School of Music of the University of Edinburgh, for his kindness in supplying me with source references together with detailed information of certain of the more obscure musical examples, and to Dr Frederick Hudson, the University, Newcastle-upon-Tyne, for much valuable information on Handel's fourth Concerto Grosso of Op. 3. I should like to express my gratitude to Dr John Reid, Professor in the English Department of my own University, who kindly undertook to read the completed typescript. His many helpful suggestions led to a number of revisions. To Professor Allwyn Keys, Head of the Department of Romance Languages, and to my children, Rosemary and David, go my thanks for their help with translations. My special thanks are due to Mrs Marta Borowska, Head of the Interloan Department of the University Library for her untiring efforts in obtaining material on my behalf; also to the Music Department Secretary, Miss Peggy Parkinson, who kindly devoted a considerable amount of time to checking the typescript. Finally, I record the very real debt of gratitude due to my wife, Peggy, who read through the entire manuscript, making many valuable suggestions, and who gave me constant encouragement throughout the writing of this work.

University of Auckland   CHARLES NALDEN

CONTENTS

PREFACE

A suggestion that I should attempt to solve what he termed 'the riddle of the fugal answer' was put to me by the late Professor H. Hollinrake (Professor of Music, University of Auckland, 1935–55), who was already aware of my growing uneasiness with most text-books' explanation of this particular aspect of fugue.

The student of fugue scarcely need be reminded how deep-rooted this feeling of uneasiness is. Dissatisfaction with the existing order of things has nowhere been more forcibly expressed, perhaps, than by the early-nineteenth-century French theorist, H. R. Colet: 'Great arguments have arisen in our schools on the true solution for an answer, but authorities have rarely agreed. . . . This passion for the answer is so great that certain composers are still spending their lives seeking the solution for answers which are difficult to contrive. We advise the student not to imitate them; this is not real composition.'[1]

Colet also relates the following story, which is both amusing and revealing:

Here is a story Reicha once told his class. He had given as an examination fugue subject the following

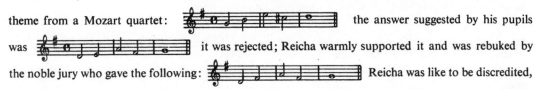

theme from a Mozart quartet: the answer suggested by his pupils was it was rejected; Reicha warmly supported it and was rebuked by the noble jury who gave the following: Reicha was like to be discredited,

when he had the Mozart quartet brought, and proved to them that the great master whom they all worshipped, had done as the students had done. It was then Reicha's turn to exult over their discomfiture and probably a joy for him to humiliate a band of infallible scholars, who even after his death did not cease their attacks upon him. Nevertheless we do not support Reicha when he gives several answers to the same subject.[2]

Although we may smile at this account, the dispute is typical of the conflicting views (albeit not so colourfully expressed) that have constantly beset the answer.

If we accept the opinion of the writer of the article *Fugue* in Stainer and Barrett's *Dictionary of Musical Terms*, we can only conclude that the 'riddle of the fugal answer' had come no nearer a solution by the end of the nineteenth century than in Colet's day: 'Many writers have attempted to draw up a regular code of laws, but the exceptions which persistently come forward render them almost useless.'[3] Nearer our own times, the late Sir Donald Tovey complained, 'The rules governing details of tonal answers are vexatious.'[4] Some few years later came a highly provocative discussion on the answer by George Oldroyd.[5]

A more recent writer, Imogene Horsley, expresses the view, 'There are few fields in the study of music in which the complexities of theoretical rationalization and musical logic are so intricate and frustrating as in the study of the fugal answer.'[6]

Such is the nature of the subject.

---

[1] H. R. Colet, *La panharmonie musicale*, Paris, 1837, pp. 236–7.
[2] Anton Reicha (1770–1836), theorist and composer. Author of *Traité de haute composition musicale*, Paris, 1824–26.
[3] London, 1898, p. 189.
[4] D. F. Tovey, *Musical Textures*, London, 1941, p. 25.
[5] G. Oldroyd, *The Technique and Spirit of Fugue*, London, 1948, Chap. 5.
[6] I. Horsley, *Fugue— History and Practice*, New York, 1966, p. 116.

The main body of this work examines the tonal answer against the background of modern theory. Although reference is made to several textbooks, the investigation is centred mainly on Prout's *Fugue*. This is because this work stands at the end of a long line of textbooks on the subject intended for the classroom rather than for the composer. Prout's two comprehensive chapters on the answer must have seemed at the time of their appearance to have said all that there was to be said on the matter. His conclusions are the result of a critical examination of the theoretical works of certain other writers from the mid-eighteenth century onwards, together with his own research into the music of the same period. Subsequent writers such as Gédalge, Macpherson, and Kitson appear to owe so much to Prout for the source of several of their rules on the answer, that his *Fugue* spontaneously suggested itself as the logical point of departure for an investigation of this nature. Finally, there can be little doubt that Prout's influence is still strongly felt, for almost seventy years following its publication, his *Fugue* could still be applauded as 'still better than any rivals, English or continental'.[7]

Although at times the degree of criticism (particularly of Prout's chapters on the Answer) may appear somewhat severe, and too much in line with the current trend of discrediting the work of certain nineteenth- and early-twentieth-century theorists,[8] I make the plea that such criticism be not mistaken for unkindness on my part. In self-defence I would point out that as the main purpose of this work is to examine objectively the various aspects of fugal answer against the background of the standard textbooks' approach, such criticism becomes unavoidable.

A consequence of this is the admittedly liberal amount of quotation from the standard textbooks. As, in the main, each quotation is used as a basis for the ensuing argument, I make the further plea that this too is unavoidable; for it is difficult to see how else the several arguments could possibly be developed. Quotation is thus an integral part of the text.

This brings me to the main purpose of the work—a direct challenge to the generally accepted approach to what is perhaps the most contentious aspect of fugal theory, the answer.

Most misunderstandings of the principle of Baroque fugal answer appear to have arisen from one of two causes—failure to take into consideration the limitations of contemporaneous harmonic practice, and failure to perceive the possible effect of a movement's overall tonal design upon an answer's shape.

I have endeavoured to prove that the seemingly capricious behaviour of so many 'irregular' answers has its explanation in terms of one or the other of these two aspects.

Connected with this is the basic error of criticizing the answer in isolation from the general context. For example, the tonal design of, say, a fugal gigue, which may require a certain delaying of dominant tonality in its first part, might well be the determining factor behind a seemingly irregular answer. An actual instance of this is quoted in Chapter VI (Ex. 138, pp. 147-8).

From the student's viewpoint, matters have been made no easier by the average textbook's practice of quoting subject and answer out of their harmonized context. In turn, this practice has had the effect of fostering the idea that a critical study of fugal answer should be based upon purely melodic considerations. In reality, nothing is further from the truth. The quoting of subject and answer out of their harmonized context tells

---

[7] A. Hutchings, *The Invention and Composition of Music*, London, 1958, p. 215.
[8] It tends sometimes to be forgotten that, in writing his numerous textbooks, Prout, after all, was only meeting a demand (and that in an astonishingly industrious and comprehensive manner) by the English musical scholar of his day. One of the current misgivings voiced against Prout's textbooks in general, is their voluminous detail and their over-preoccupation with rules. Here again, it is doubtful whether textbooks of any less preponderous proportions would have satisfied most musical scholars of Prout's day.

us nothing, whereas my own research into the matter has convinced me, at any rate, that by examining these joint aspects, subject and answer in full context, many an otherwise inexplicable situation is made clear. How else, for example, could one explain away Handel's unusual answer in *Dixit Dominus* (Ex. 172a, p. 178) except that by answering the subject as he does, he gains his point, which is retention of tonic tonality for well-nigh half the course of the 120 or so bars' final fugue? Or take the subject and answer of the same composer's *Capriccio* (Ex. 119, p. 107). Here, Handel's answer flouts on several occasions the textbook rule, that the answer should reproduce exactly the interval sequence of the subject, tone for tone, semitone for semitone, and so on. An answer given under these conditions must inevitably introduce subdominant tonality, a tonality that Handel studiously avoids throughout the movement, limiting what modulation there is to the 'sharp side' of the tonic.

Examined in isolation, Handel's answer would appear unnecessarily perverse, but examined in *full context*, his purpose, that of limiting tonality to a predetermined tonal design, is made clear. Hence the unsoundness of basing criticism upon purely melodic considerations.

In short, these two particular answers are not free agents, in that their shapes are determined by preconceived considerations of their respective movements' overall tonal designs.

Although the number of supporting examples may appear somewhat excessive, I would point out that one cannot expect to establish new theories, which in some cases run directly counter to the old, on the strength of a few isolated examples. Further supporting examples, far too numerous to quote, could have been added.

PART I

INTRODUCTION

THE ORIGIN AND NATURE OF THE TONAL ANSWER

Opinion is sharply divided regarding the origin and nature of the tonal (melodically altered) fugal answer, as distinguished from the real (melodically identical) answer. Some trace the origin of the tonal answer to modal times, viewing its continued appearance in the Baroque as nothing more than a lingering modal custom, whereas others, although tracing its origin possibly to modal procedure, link the increasing frequency of its use with the gradual feeling on the part of the sixteenth-century composer for major-minor tonality.

Prout subscribes to the former view when he writes: 'We have already shown that the tonal answer is the result of the old modal systems which prevailed before modern tonality, as now understood, was fixed.'[1]

This same view is taken by George Oldroyd: 'In the translation of music ... from the modes to our keys, the art of musical thinking was changed . . . and although modal thought, modal tonality, was gradually left behind, yet the modal habits of thinking and working lingered on, in fact, were much alive, and had influence on the habits of thinking and working in our major and minor scales.'[2]

A little later in the same chapter, Oldroyd specifically relates the tonal answer to the modal period, and the real answer to the period of our major-minor tonality:

'Thus in Mode I a subject commencing on the Final . . . would be answered by its dominant. But if it commenced on A the dominant, it would not be answered by E the fifth above but by D the fourth above . . . because D being the Final defines the mode at the very outset, whereas E would not.

'Nevertheless, were this being regarded as an answer in A minor to a subject in D minor there is no reason whatever why this E should not be the right note other than the keeping of this modal tradition . . .'[3]

Oldroyd's reasoning here is again in direct line with that of Prout, who writes: 'it is quite evident that in many cases the great composers felt this to be of much more importance than the keeping of an old rule [the rule of tonal answer] which was made before modern tonality was established.'[4]

Gustave Reese, on the other hand, links the increasing frequency of its use with the increasing feeling of the sixteenth-century composer for major-minor tonality. These composers, he says, 'were increasingly attracted to tonal, or quasi-tonal, answers, the more they abandoned the relics of the modal system and veered toward major and minor'.[5]

This assumption is lent support by Lowinsky:

Although Josquin and his contemporaries made a fundamental contribution to tonality in terms of the use of the major mode, of tonal harmony, and of tonal unity throughout a large work, they used the tonal answer in fugal imitation only sporadically. Palestrina's motets show increasing concern with this aspect of tonality. In his first motet book (1563) only two works transform the interval of a fourth in the

---

[1] E. Prout, *Fugue*, London, 1891, p. 40, para. 100.
[2] *Technique and Spirit*, p. 64.
[3] p. 71.
[4] *Fugue*, p. 46, para. 108.
[5] G. Reese, *Music in the Renaissance*, New York, 1959, p. 351.

dux to that of the fifth in the *comes*, thus rounding out the octave and keeping subject and answer within the confines of one mode. A surprisingly high number of motets starting out with the interval of a fourth or a fifth have real answers. This proportion is almost reversed in Palestrina's motet book of 1569, in which only two compositions that begin with the interval of a fourth or a fifth have real answers, whereas no fewer than seven works have tonal answers. On the whole, the tonal answer occurs with increasing frequency in Palestrina's works, but the real answer by no means disappears. Tonal and real answer coexist in most of his later prints on a basis of artistic and often even numerical equality.

Willaert's nine instrumental *ricercari a 3*, however, have four works with tonal answer. . . . It is interesting that Zarlino, Willaert's disciple, in his two-part examples illustrating the twelve modes should use tonal answers in each example that starts with the interval of a fifth or with a triadic motif. This corroborates, I believe, a thesis propounded in a discussion of the fantasias of Charles Guillet (Paris, 1610) to the effect that the origin of the tonal answer lies in the old 'division of the authentic modes into a group of five and four tones . . . and that of their plagal companions into groups of four and five . . .'[6]

Although not directly expressing this same view, Jeppeson at least lends support to Reese's contention that the increasing frequency in the use of tonal answer moved uniformly with the transition from mode to scale when he writes:

'Tonal imitation was especially popular in the seventeenth and eighteenth centuries. With Bach and Handel, tonal imitation was the usual procedure.

'In the sixteenth century, on the other hand, the real answer to a subject was preferred.'[7]

The two views are thus diametrically opposed. In short, whereas Prout and Oldroyd regard the appearance of tonal answer from the seventeenth century onwards as a survival of a modal custom, Reese does not link it with modal procedure so much as with the gradual feeling of the sixteenth-century composer for major-minor tonality; and although Lowinsky supports the view of Prout and Oldroyd in attributing the *origin* of tonal answer to the distinction between the authentic and plagal forms of a mode, he nevertheless follows Reese in linking the increasing frequency of its use with the gradual move towards the major-minor tonal system.

Which view is correct—that of Prout and Oldroyd on the one hand, or Reese and Lowinsky on the other—poses a question of fundamental importance, in that its outcome could well be the means of opening the way for a full understanding of the whole principle of fugal answer, particularly in its reference to seventeenth and eighteenth century practice.

Our first task therefore is to examine the two claims.

In passing, it should perhaps be pointed out that the question of where the actual origin of the tonal answer lies is not the real concern of a work of this nature; the work's real concern is with the tonal answer's subsequent course, its purpose and nature.

[6] E. E. Lowinsky, *Tonality and Atonality in Sixteenth-Century Music*, Berkeley, 1961, pp. 31–32.
[7] K. Jeppeson, *Counterpoint*, London, 1950, p. 163.

CHAPTER I

FUGAL ANSWER IN THEORY

1. *THE FIFTEENTH AND SIXTEENTH CENTURIES*

It is an accepted tradition that a fugue subject is answered either at the fifth above or the fourth below, or, more rarely, at the fourth above or the fifth below. The former is termed a dominant, and the latter a subdominant answer.

The fugal answer has its origin in the imitative technique of Renaissance vocal polyphony, which accounts for the choice of the fourth and fifth as intervals of reply, for these mark the approximate distances between adjacent vocal registers—alto from soprano, tenor from alto, and so on.

The first to recommend the fourth, fifth, and octave for imitative entries, apparently, was the fifteenth-century theorist, Bartolomé Ramos de Pareja: 'However, the best method of composing is when the second part imitates the melodic line of the subject. It makes its entry not simultaneously, but after one or several notes, and does so either with the same theme at the same pitch, or with a similar theme at the fourth or fifth, or even the octave. . . . Practising musicians call this method "fugue", because one voice follows another with similar arsis or thesis.'[1]

It is interesting to find another theorist some three-quarters of a century later recording his strong preference for imitative entries at the fourth or fifth in favour of those at the unison and octave:

'And good fugues may be constructed in various ways, but not by the unison, nor by the octave since these do not give enough variety. This way of constructing fugues by unison and octave should not be resorted to frequently, except in case of necessity. And when the bass of a four-part fugue imitates the tenor at the fourth, the alto and soprano will enter at the fifth; and conversely when the bass and tenor imitate each other at the fifth, the alto and soprano will imitate each other at the fourth.'[2]

More important to our study is Vicentino's observation concerning the construction of fugues by contrary motion: 'And when one part leaps down by a fifth, the other must leap up by a fourth; and when one part leaps down by a fourth, the other must leap up by a fifth, so that the octave may be correctly formed.'[3]

Thus we see emerging, apparently for the first time in musical theory, the foundation principle of the tonal answer. Here it is concerned only with fugue by contrary motion, but in both this, and in his observations concerning alternating imitative entries at the fourth and fifth, we see Vicentino drawing attention to the unequal division of the scale (of a fourth answering a fifth, and vice versa) as a means of confining successive entries within the octave limits of a mode's outer finals. Definition of mode was thus accomplished by the cross-answering of its two most characteristic notes, final and dominant. These two notes were pivotal, and marked the structural divisions between the authentic and plagal forms of a mode, in that the former divided into a pentachord plus a tetrachord, pivoting on the dominant, the latter reversing this process, and pivoting on the final:

[1] Ramos de Pareja, *Musica Practica*, ed. J. Wolf, Leipzig, 1901, p. 68.
[2] N. Vicentino, *L'Antica Musica ridotta alla moderna prattica*, Rome, 1555, p. 88.
[3] pp. 88–89.

B

Ex. 1.

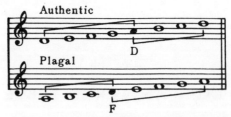

Ultimately from this came the rule, from the seventeenth century onwards, that a leap from final to dominant should be answered tonally by a leap from dominant to final, and, conversely, that a leap from dominant to final should be answered tonally by a leap from final to dominant. A tonal answer was frequently given when final and dominant were in relatively close proximity:

Ex. 2. BYRD, MOTET, HAEC DIES

Furthermore, the response to a 'subject' commencing on a mode's dominant, would almost invariably commence on the same mode's final, whence arose the origin of the subdominant answer. Definition of a mode through its final and dominant thus became accomplished at the very outset of a composition.

Following closely upon Vicentino's *L'Antica Musica ridotta alla moderna prattica*, came Zarlino's great work *Istitutioni harmoniche* (1558); but although Zarlino recognizes the intervals for fugal entries as the unison, fourth, fifth and octave (taking care at the same time to distinguish between fugue and imitation whose intervals of reply are not thus restricted),[4] and although his two-part examples illustrating the twelve modes include instances of final and dominant cross-answering each other,[5] he does not follow up Vicentino's rule relating to fugue by contrary motion, and neither does he make any new rule pertaining to the normal form of tonal answer which was being used so freely in contemporary composition.

The last Renaissance work to be discussed is *A Plaine and Easie Introduction to Practicall Musicke*[6] by the English composer and theorist, Thomas Morley. Although both his own work and that of his English contemporaries provide abundant proof of their familiarity with the tonal answer, Morley does not discuss it beyond distinguishing between canon and imitation:

Ex. 3. MORLEY, FROM A PLAINE AND EASIE INTRODUCTION

[4] G. Zarlino, *Istitutioni harmoniche*, Venice, 1589, Part III, Chap. 54, p. 270.
[5] Part IV, Chap. 18 *et. seq*.
[6] T. Morley, *A Plaine and Easie Introduction to Practicall Musicke*, ed. A. Harman, London, 1952.

Philomathes: This riseth five notes and the plainsong riseth but four.

Master: So did you in your example before, although you could perceive it in mine and not in your own; but although it rise five notes yet is it the point, for if it were in canon we might not rise one note higher nor descend one note lower than the plainsong did, but in imitations we are not so straitly bound.[7]

Vicentino's rule relating to fugal answer by contrary motion excepted, Morley's *A Plaine and Easie Introduction* is thus in line with other Renaissance theoretical works, in that it does not discuss the fugal aspect of tonal answer.

The possible significance of this is now discussed.

2. THE SEVENTEENTH CENTURY

It is no mere coincidence, one feels, that the stricter application from now on of the tonal answer coincides with the gradual supersession of the modes by our modern major-minor scalic system. Furthermore, the awareness by theorists of practice is evidenced by the inclusion in all major theoretical writings of the rule of tonal answer relating to the cross-answering of tonic and dominant by dominant and tonic, and vice versa. Dr Jeppeson's assertion that 'the composers of the sixteenth century at times used the tonal answer, but that they, as a rule, preferred the real form',[8] is rather too broad a statement, for as we shall see, this preference for real answers was more strongly marked in Palestrina than in the contemporary English School. If we accept this to be correct, plus the fact that major-minor tonality manifested itself decidedly earlier in the music of the English composers of this period than in that of their Italian contemporaries, and add Jeppeson's further observation that 'tonal imitation was especially popular in the seventeenth and eighteenth centuries',[9] then the total sum of evidence strongly suggests that the transition from mode to scale moved uniformly with a more consistent application of the tonal answer. Finally, as Jeppeson points out, 'With Bach and Handel, tonal imitation was the usual procedure'.[10]

What had the appearance of being somewhat tentative in the writings of Renaissance theorists, now became decidedly more positive, for as early as 1650 we see Christoph Bernhard (who eventually succeeded his teacher Schütz as Kapellmeister at Dresden) giving direct guidance in the matter of fugal answer. For this purpose, Bernhard uses the terms *consociatio modorum* and *aequatio modorum*, the former embracing the principle of tonal answer, and the latter of real answer:

The *consociatio modorum* is a combination of the authentic with its plagal, and of the plagal with its authentic in two, three, or more voices adjacent to one another.

As the Cantus is an octave removed from the Tenor, it happens commonly that they are both of one mode. On the other hand, as the Alto and Bass differ from the Tenor by a fourth or fifth, and keep the distance of an octave between them, they are commonly of a different Mode from the Tenor, and of the same kind as each other in such a way that:

When the Tenor is of the first mode, it has it in common with the Cantus; but if the Bass is of the second mode, and likewise the Alto, and vice versa, if the Tenor is of the second mode, the Discant is of the same pitch with it, but the other two are of the first mode.

Consociatio is the best way of contriving Fugues in all voices according to the mode, especially when the subjects do not exceed the fourth and fifth, and have a comfortable leap. For this purpose the fourth is transformed into a fifth, and the fifth into a fourth, and where possible the semitones are retained since they are also important notes as may be seen from the following examples over all modes.[11]

---

[7] p.151.
[8] *Counterpoint,* p. 266.
[9] p. 163.
[10] p. 163.
[11] C. Bernhard, *Tractatus compositionis augmentatus,* ed. J. M. Müller-Blattau, Leipzig, 1926, p. 98.

Before going on to discuss *aequatio modorum* he introduces a cautionary note: 'One should not deviate too much at the beginning from this procedure; in the middle however it is not taken so literally.'[12]

Aequatio modorum (real answer) is then discussed: 'This method of Fugue is more used in "passages of leaps", more in the middle than at the beginning.'

Two features, important to this discussion, stand out in Bernhard's work. First, as Dr Mann points out: 'In Bernhard's work, the study of fugue forms part of a new interpretation of modal theory which approaches the system of major and minor tonalities. He adopts the mode based on C as the first, "since all others follow its model in their perfect cadences" '.[13] And second, his advice as to when and where one should use real and tonal answers. In effect, Bernhard advocates a firmly established tonality at the very outset through the device of tonal answer, which once accomplished, leaves the composer less 'straitly bound', so that 'in the repetition the fourth may remain a fourth and the fifth a fifth'. It was to find an echo in Rameau's famous *Traité de l'harmonie* some three-quarters of a century later.

In all these matters Bernhard appears truly prophetic, for his structural plan regarding the distribution of real and tonal answers, and the effect of the latter upon clear definition of tonality have been in evidence ever since. Textbook strictures notwithstanding, in the Bach-Handel period, the tonal answer principle at the commencement of the work was 'not easily deviated from'.

No less emphatic about entries at the octave and fifth, and the rule of tonal answer between final and dominant and vice versa, is the French theorist, Guillaume Gabriel Nivers (1617–1714), whose *Traité de la composition* appeared in the same year as that in which he became organist to the King, 1667. His *Traité* advises that:

> To construct a fugue, three things must be considered, its beginning, its continuation, and its ending.
> It should commence on the degree of the final, or on the dominant, rarely on the mediant of the key in which one is writing.
> It should proceed through the essential notes of the key directly or indirectly. Directly, for example, if it begins on the final, it should proceed by ascending a third or a fifth, or by descending a fourth. If it begins on the dominant, it should proceed, if ascending, by a fourth and if descending, by a third or fifth. Indirectly, for example, when it proceeds by conjunct degrees with the intention nevertheless of passing directly through the essential notes of the key.
> If the subject (that is the first part that begins the fugue) commences on the final, the second part should commence on the dominant; and conversely if the one begins with the dominant, the other should begin on the final.
> If the subject proceeds by a fifth, the second part should proceed by a fourth; conversely if the subject proceeds by a fourth, the second part should proceed by a fifth.
> The third part entering to take up the fugue, does the same as the first, and the fourth as the second, and so on alternately. Nevertheless, this order is not always observed, for two successive parts may well take up the fugue in the same way, [14] and it is of no importance to which part the subject is given; that is, the fugue may begin with the Soprano, Alto, Tenor, or even Bass, and thereafter introduce any part you like.[15]

This extract is interesting in several ways. It contains one of the earliest appearances of the terms 'final' and 'dominant'[16] where they relate specifically to fugal entries. It lays a

[12] p. 102.
[13] A. Mann, *The Study of Fugue*, New Brunswick, N.J., 1958, p. 38.
[14] Prout terms such expositions 'irregular'. (*Fugue*, p. 89, para. 206.)
[15] G. G. Nivers, *Traité de la composition de musique*, Paris, 1667, pp. 49–51.
[16] Salomon de Caus was the first writer, apparently, to draw attention to contemporary usage of the term dominant: 'and as for the note comprised within the octave, called by some modern writers the *dominant note*, it should be sounded often, in order to conform with the nature of the mode containing the said note. For it is the one that usually distinguishes the mode you wish to represent.' (*Institution harmonique*, Frankfurt, 1615, Chap. X, p. 21.)

secure foundation for the justification of the subdominant answer. ('If the one begins with the dominant, the other should begin on the final.') It gives the layout of a complete fugal exposition, but is not so dogmatic as to insist upon a rigid alternation of entries between final and dominant.

Before the close of the century we find the term 'mode' discarded in favour of 'key'. This is in John Playford's *Introduction to the Art of Descant*. The edition printed in 1697 acknowledges the 'Additions of the late Mr Henry Purcell'. His chapter on 'Fuge, or Pointing' opens with a description of fugue: 'A *Fuge* is, when one Part leads one, two, three, four or more Notes, and the other repeats the same in the *Unison*, or such like in the *Octave*, a *Fourth* or *Fifth* above or below the Leading Part.'[17]

Thus the unison, octave, fourth and fifth are now firmly established as the only intervals of reply. Playford's next observation establishes no less firmly the function and purpose of the tonal answer: 'Observe in this Example [Ex. 4], that the *Treble* rises a *Fifth*, and the *Bass* but a *Fourth*, which is done, because it relates more to the *Key* than rising a *Fifth*. So all *Fuges* of this nature are to be manag'd, if done Masterly.'[18]

Ex. 4. PLAYFORD, FROM AN INTRODUCTION TO THE ART OF DESCANT

We may pause at this point with the purpose of finding out exactly what was implied by the term 'fugue'. For an explanation of this, we are again indebted to Purcell, for he makes it quite clear that the term 'fugue' does not imply a form, but the technical style of a composition: 'Most of these different sorts of *Fugeing* are used in *Sonata's*, the chiefest Instrumental *Musick* now in request, where you will find *Double* and *Treble Fuges* also reverted and augmented in their *Canzona's*, with a great deal of Art mixed with good Air, which is the Perfection of a Master.'[19]

What we should not overlook is the vast difference between the application of fugal technique in sixteenth and seventeenth century composition. Whereas fugue in the sixteenth century seldom exceeded the modern equivalent of a fugal exposition, by the close of the seventeenth century it is a commonplace to find a single fugue subject sufficing for the construction of an extended movement. Moreover, the now firmly established major-minor tonality shows orientation from the style of the Renaissance to be virtually complete.

3. THE EIGHTEENTH CENTURY

Rameau devotes the final chapter of his *Traité de l'harmonie* (1722) to a discussion of fugal technique, but although he quotes a number of seemingly hard and fast rules, he is at pains on more than one occasion to stress their arbitrary character; thus in his concluding paragraph: 'A Fugue is an Ornament in Music, founded upon good Taste; so that the most general Rules we have given, are hardly sufficient to succeed perfectly in it. The various Sentiments and Events that can be expressed in Music, introduce every Moment a Novelty which cannot be reduced to fixed Rules.'[20]

[17] J. Playford, *An Introduction to the Art of Descant*, add. by H. Purcell, London, 1697, p. 96.
[18] p. 97.
[19] p. 115.
[20] J. P. Rameau, *Traité de l'harmonie*, ed. J. French, London, c. 1775, Chap. XLIV, p. 176.

Rameau's explanation of the tonal answer is careful and detailed, particularly so of the type of subject that proceeds scalewise between dominant and tonic: 'Many Things are to be observed to avoid Mistakes in the Choice (which appears to be arbitrary) between each of the five Notes from the Key to the Fifth ascending, in order to make an Air answerable to that of the four Notes from the Fifth to the Key-note ascending, whether the Air ascends or descends; for there will always be found five Notes one Way, and four on the other.'[21]

There is scarcely need to reproduce Rameau's first five supporting examples, which are all elementary illustrations of the point he has just made. Here however is his Sixth Example:

Ex. 5A. RAMEAU, FROM TRAITÉ DE L'HARMONIE

Ex. 5B. IBID.

It will be seen that the dominant (A) in bar two of Ex. 5a is given a real answer, and in Ex. 5b a tonal one. What accounts for the real reply in Ex. 5a? The reason, I suggest, is that this particular melodic pattern does not lend itself kindly to mutation without undue distortion of its melodic line. Consider the experiments in Ex. 6a and 6b.

Ex. 6A.

Ex. 6B.

Neither of these is wholly satisfactory. The distortion in 6a needs no further comment. In 6b, the melodic line is now far too removed from the shapely contour of the original.

Analysis and discussion of this particular example (5a) have been prolonged deliberately, because it is by no means an isolated case of its kind. Indeed, subjects with a similar melodic pattern are fairly plentiful, and discussion will be renewed in a later chapter.

[21] p. 160.

The second part of Rameau's example (5b) demonstrates that a subdominant answer from its second note onwards is the only satisfactory way of replying tonally to the subject's dominant (A).

The first part of Rameau's example (Ex. 5a) in which the dominant note is not replied to tonally, provides an instance of the claim of tonal answer giving way to a more important musical consideration. But it was 'exceptions to the rule' such as this, that led later theorists mistakenly to suggest that with the decay of the modal system the 'old rule', as they termed it, no longer held good.

Prout for example writes:

'This is a good rule enough, if it were only observed . . .

'quite enough examples will be found in which it is broken to show that they did not regard it as one of the laws of the Medes and Persians.'[22]

As has already been suggested, stricter conformity to the rule of tonal answer developed alongside the gradual ousting of the modes by the major-minor scalic system; but departures from the rule notwithstanding, late seventeenth and eighteenth century practice viewed the procedure as relatively strict. It is understandable that situations involving more important considerations, such as those of tonality, were bound to arise rendering a tonal answer impracticable. But such departures from the rule did not, as Prout appears to imply, prove that it was dead; neither, as he also appears to imply, was the rule strictly observed prior to Bach and Handel. We have to look no further than Purcell's Sonata No. 7 of *Sonatas of Four Parts* to see how, on occasion, the rule would at times give way to more important musical considerations:

Ex. 7.   PURCELL, TEN SONATAS OF FOUR PARTS, No. 7

As Purcell himself quotes the rule of tonal answer, Ex. 7 makes it quite obvious that it never had been regarded as 'one of the Laws of the Medes and Persians'. Exceptions such as this do not weaken the assertion that from the seventeenth century onwards it was regarded as a relatively strict basic procedure. But more of this in a later chapter.

Fux's famous *Gradus ad Parnassum*[23] (1725) followed closely upon Rameau's *Traité*. Its discussion will come later.

---

[22] *Fugue*, p. 33, paras. 86–87.
[23] Although not strictly relevant to our main discussion, it may not be out of place to draw attention to a curious inaccuracy concerning Fux's *Gradus* and its alleged influence on Bach's fugal style, which so far, apparently, has been allowed to pass unchallenged:

'It was the text-book of Fux (1725) which placed the fugue on its present basis, though still in a very simple and undeveloped form. Thus the way was prepared for J. S. Bach, who took the fugue as set forth in Fux's *Gradus ad Parnassum* and applied to it the new key-system with its endless possibilities of modulation, enriching it at the same time with his boundless wealth of melodic and harmonic imagination. Bach rose superior to all the rules and regulations with which Fux had hedged in the fugue, and evolved out of Fux's skeleton the living fugue, the quintessence of fugue, freed from all the impurities of pedantry.' (*Grove's Dictionary of Music and Musicians*, 5th ed., London, 1954, III, p. 514.)

This is completely opposed to fact, and detracts (unintentionally no doubt) from Bach's originality. Jeppeson is to the point when he writes in the Preface to his *Counterpoint* 'to this type of polyphony [Bach's polyphony] the work of Fux could not lead, nor was it intended that it should', which is little different from Spitta's remark, 'Hence, notwithstanding his [Bach's] approval of Fux's method, it was only natural for him to prefer another style of instruction. That was very well fitted for vocal compositions . . . it could not be used for the instruction of writers for the organ or clavier, since it placed the learner in direct opposition to the demands of his instrument.' (P. Spitta, *Johann Sebastian Bach*, trans. Clara Bell and J. A. Fuller-Maitland, New York, 1951, Vol. III, pp. 125–6.)

These observations apart, it need only be pointed out that the great series of organ fugues of Bach's Weimar period had been completed at least eight years before the *Gradus* made its appearance.

9

We now pass on to Johann Mattheson's *Der vollkommene Capellmeister* (1739). Paul Henry Lang draws attention to 'an entirely new era of musical thought' that emerged during the early years of the eighteenth century, and its subsequent effect upon the teaching of music theory.

'Beginning with Mattheson the philosophical conceptions and empirical leanings of the Enlightenment began to displace entirely the many medieval survivals still extant in earlier baroque musical thought. In his very first work, *Das Neu-Eröffnete Orchestre* (1713), the tendency to turn to the educated music lover instead of to the professional musician is apparent.'[24]

Mattheson's role as it affects this discussion is expanded upon rather more fully by Alfred Mann, who writes:

Yet, though Mattheson's discussion of fugue moves on familiar ground, it is guided by a spirit markedly different from that of earlier theoretical works. Mattheson is the first author who does not address his instruction to the 'young composer' but rather to the 'professional and amateur'—*Kenner und Leibhaber*. Mattheson's intention is clearly stated in a remark with which he shortens the discussion of fugue in his first musical treatise, *Das neueröffnete Orchestre* (1713): 'My purpose, however, is not so much to train the composer as to offer my help to the amateur who wishes to form a judgement of things musical but needs no *mysteria* of this kind.' . . . Mattheson's approach to fugal instruction was obviously prompted by the increasing lay interest in the art of music. The new situation of musical practice with which he was confronted is easily understood from his mention of the music lover who plays a fugue well but does not know of what it consists. Yet, addressing primarily the connoisseur rather than the creative artist, Mattheson's writing introduced a critical change in the teaching of composition—a change from living music to an inanimate subject. It was bound to prepare the ground for theoretical literature which taught 'a métier, not an art.'[25]

What must not be lost sight of is Mattheson's own declared angle of approach; for although at times his rules pertaining to fugal answer, like those of Purcell, Rameau, and Fux before him, run counter in many respects to contemporaneous practice, it would be absurd to suggest that Mattheson, musician and scholar, was so out of touch with things as not to be alive to this. Indeed, this may be claimed to hold good of all the great theorists such as Fux, Marpurg, Albrechtsberger, and Cherubini, whose respective compositions testify that outside the classroom their rules never were expected to be interpreted literally.

What has happened is simply that a distinction has now been drawn between so-called 'students'' and 'composers'' fugue.[26] Discussion of the merits or demerits of this conception is beyond the scope of a work of this nature, except to point out that so far as fugal answer is concerned it is from these times that we can trace a stiffening attitude on the part of the theorist, resulting in turn in a considerable loss of freedom when it came to devising an answer to a fugue subject.

Had this purely scholastic approach (which bore little relation to practice) continued to be confined to the classroom, all might still have been well, and the many difficulties and contradictions which continue to cloud clear understanding of the Baroque principle of tonal answer would never have arisen; but, as we shall see, apparent misunderstanding of these earlier theorists' intentions led later theorists to criticize adversely Baroque and Classical composers' works from the standpoint of these purely academic criteria.

An example of this stiffening attitude is seen in Mattheson's chapter on the Answer in *Der vollkommene Capellmeister*. Following a number of examples illustrating various

---

[24] P. H. Lang, *Music in Western Civilisation*, New York, 1941, p. 440.
[25] *The Study of Fugue*, pp. 54–55.
[26] Cherubini for example makes this distinction: 'All these combinations may be employed, and still more, in a study-fugue; but there should be a judicious selection of them, in a fugue intended for the public.' L. Cherubini, *A Treatise on Counterpoint and Fugue*, trans. Cowden Clarke, London, 1854, p. 63.

ways of replying tonally to subjects in which tonic and dominant are involved, he sums up by saying: 'It may be seen clearly and in all cases, that in regular answers the fourth becomes a fifth, and the fifth a fourth. . . . And the seventh theme shows in the answer not only that the steps must be halved, but also that the falling second must become a unison, whether the subject begin on the dominant or the tonic.'[27]

Ex. 8A.   MATTHESON, FROM DER VOLLKOMMENE CAPELLMEISTER

Ex. 8B.   IBID.

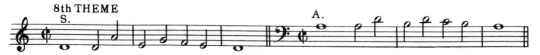

Realizing that in both these cases respect for rule does not result in wholly satisfactory answers, Mattheson continues: 'If the all too regular answers, e.g. Nos. 7 and 8 as here [i.e. Ex. 8a and 8b] have a certain lameness in the melody, then for the sake of correctness, one must rest content *the first time* with a regular fugue; but *after that*, the composer is free to arrange the sequence in such a way that it may sound more natural.'[28]

Ex. 8C.   IBID.

Ex. 8D.   IBID.

Mattheson thus recommends the keeping of a rule for its own sake ('for the sake of correctness'), and that in preference to what he himself admits to being the more musically satisfying answer. Even so, cases such as this should be reconciled with Mattheson's intended purpose, for the general style of both the text and the musical illustrations (whose scholastic severity is as far removed in style from composition in his own day as it is possible to be) makes it plain that such rules are specifically designed to reach out to the uninitiated.

Furthermore, there can be little doubt of Mattheson's awareness of the fact that his 'regular' answer, although theoretically 'correct', was not altogether in keeping with general contemporary practice, where similarly constructed subjects were concerned; for this pattern (as in Ex. 8a) which consists of an unbroken scale-line running up from tonic to dominant, was normally given a real reply, the relatively close proximity of tonic and dominant notes notwithstanding. Examples that readily come to mind are Handel,

[27] J. Mattheson, *Der vollkommene Capellmeister*, Hamburg, 1739, p. 372, para. 37.
[28] p. 372, para. 38.

Concerto Grosso, Op. 6, No. 10 in D minor, and the *Amen* chorus from *Messiah*; Bach, 'Forty-Eight', Book II,[29] No. 10 in E minor, and the D minor Clavier Toccata;[30] and Pachelbel, *Interludes to the Magnificat*, V.3, V.4.[31]

More enlightened, insofar as choice of illustrative material is concerned, is Marpurg's *Abhandlung von der Fuge* (1753–4) whose text is supported by a profusion of musical examples drawn from the works of earlier composers, and from those of his nearer contemporaries.

George Oldroyd is thus inaccurate, and does Marpurg an injustice, when he writes: 'I would add to Fux, Albrechtsberger, and Cherubini, another writer, Marpurg, who also did not deign to refer to Bach's methods or works in the treatise he published in 1753, which was a summary of the whole science of Counterpoint at that period.'[32] For this work draws extensively from Bach for its musical illustrations. And far from ignoring Bach's methods, Marpurg concludes the section on vocal fugue with a detailed analysis of the *Kyrie* from Bach's G major Mass,[33] paying at the same time a graceful tribute to the composer: 'It is sufficient to know the name of its illustrious author to regard it as a model in this mode of writing.'[34]

Marpurg's rules pertaining to the answer are a synthesis of those of Rameau and Mattheson, and at times he makes no attempt to disguise the fact. For example, his phrase 'It is necessary to pay more attention to what follows than to what precedes',[35] resembles too closely Rameau's 'having Regard rather to what follows than to what precedes'[36] to leave any doubt as to the source of his rules. Similarly, he sees fit to reproduce Ex. 5a and 5b (p. 8), and 8c–8d (p. 11) from Rameau and Mattheson respectively to illustrate the same points that they had already made.[37]

Marpurg's rules relating to fugal answer are thoroughly systematized, covering seemingly every manner of situation likely to be encountered in answering a subject. His chapter on the answer is clear, and its subsequent influence upon the style and form of such works as Albrechtsberger's *Gründliche Anweisung zur Composition* (1790), Prout's *Fugue* (1891) and Gédalge's *Traité de la fugue* (1901) is plain.

Even so, the gradually widening gulf separating theory from practice becomes apparent, for example, in Marpurg's rule concerning non-modulating subjects that commence on the dominant. It is mentioned here as a preamble to the general discussion of this particular aspect in a later chapter.

Ex. 9.   J. S. BACH, 'FORTY-EIGHT', BOOK II, No. 1

---

[29] Abbreviated from now on to Book I or Book II.

[30] Bach-Werke-Verzeichnis (BWV), 913 (*Presto*).

[31] See however, Thomas Attwood's *Theorie- und Kompositionsstudien bei Mozart* (W. A. Mozart, *Neue Ausgabe sämtlicher Werke*, Kassel, 1965, Series X, Vol. I, pp. 265 and 267), where the subject's scalic run from c up to g is answered on both occasions by gg–a–b–c.

[32] *Technique and Spirit*, p. 5.

[33] BWV 236.

[34] F. W. Marpurg, *Abhandlung von der Fuge*, Leipzig, edition of 1806, Part Two, Chap. VII, 18, p. 86.

[35] Part I, Chapter III 3, p. 22.

[36] *Traité*, p. 161. (This phrase forms part of both Rameau's and his own explanation of the principle of re-establishing tonic tonality in the answer to a modulating subject.)

[37] Part I, Table XXVI, figs 1 and 2; 8–10.

Between the second note of the Subject, f, and the second note of the Answer, b, a so-called fa against mi is found. This is unavoidable here, and is at least not incorrect. If it had been desired to imitate the g–f, then the Answer would have had to start with d–c, but this is contrary to the Rule. Only in the middle of a Fugue should the Answer commence on the Dominant, is it permitted to answer itself by the second degree of the principal key. It is absolutely a fundamental error at the beginning of a Fugue, and only allowed those so-called fashionable (galant) composers who permit themselves to write something whereof they can give not just cause.[38]

Although it is true that the initial note of a subject commencing on the dominant is usually replied to tonally (i.e. at the fourth and not the fifth above), sufficient examples from Palestrina onwards are quoted in Chapter IV of this work to prove that the rule never was regarded as absolute. It becomes even more difficult to reconcile this with Marpurg's strict rule when we recall that he discussed fugal technique with Bach himself, in whose work exceptions to this particular rule are not difficult to find.

A further discrepancy between theory and practice is Marpurg's rule concerning the strict observance of the interval sequence between subject and answer: 'the intervals which appeared in the Subject must appear in the Answer, and in exactly the same proportions; for example, wherever the Subject has a third, fourth, or fifth, the Answer has a third, fourth, or fifth in the corresponding place; and if a major third is used in the Subject, it must appear as such in the Answer, and so on. It means that the melodic line of the Answer must be similar to the melodic line of the Subject. This is the basic principle for the arrangement of the answer.'[39] Again we are able to find a sufficient number of examples in Bach, Handel, and others of Marpurg's contemporaries proving that the rule had absolutely no foundation in actual practice.

Here we have an example of a purely arbitrary rule, which has clung on for the best part of two centuries, and has led to such misguided strictures as 'cases could be quoted [from Bach] in which there seems to be no valid reason for the breach of the principle'.[40]

The last major theoretical work of the eighteenth century, Albrechtsberger's *Gründliche Anweisung zur Composition* (1790), provides rules relating to fugal answer closely similar to those in earlier theoretical works.

4. THE NINETEENTH CENTURY

One of the most important theoretical works on fugue to appear during the earlier part of the new century was Cherubini's *Cours de contrepoint et de la fugue* (1833) which was subsequently 'adopted for the instruction of the classes at the Conservatoire, Paris; and of those at the Royal Academy of Music, London'.[41]

Cherubini's theoretical works have long been a target for criticism, and it may be true that his severely academic style of approach bears little relation to practice. But in fairness to Cherubini, his own observations regarding the study of fugue as a scholastic discipline (i.e. as a means to an end, and not as an end in itself) should not be lost sight of:

'Such as it exists at the present time, Fugue is the perfection of counterpoint. . . .

'Fugue may be considered as the transition between the system of strict counterpoint, and that of free composition.'[42]

Furthermore, as already pointed out, Cherubini himself is careful to distinguish between a 'study-fugue', and 'fugue intended for the public'. (See p. 10, f.n. 26.)

---

[38] Part I, Chapter III, Section (Abschnitte) Two, pp. 28–29; Plate XIII, fig. 4.
[39] Part I, Chap. III, p. 21, 2.
[40] C. H. Kitson, *The Elements of Fugal Construction*, London, 1929, p. 24. This aspect (interval relationships between subject and answer) is discussed in Chap. VII of this work.
[41] Quoted from the English edition of 1854.
[42] p. 62.

With Cherubini, the tonal answer (the cross answering of tonic and dominant notes) freezes into 'the immutable rule of tonal fugue', [43] a rule which on one occasion he himself finds unable to keep: 'The subject of this fugue belongs to tonal fugue, as it descends first from the tonic to the dominant; therefore, the response should go from the dominant to the tonic. But this response would have rendered the working of the counter-subjects extremely difficult, and would have compelled frequent changes. It has been judged fit, therefore, to treat it as a real fugue.'[44]

Although worded somewhat differently from those of earlier writers on fugue, his rules governing the tonal relations between subject and answer result in imposing the same set of arbitrary restrictions:

'The Response . . . immediately follows the subject; it should be in all respects similar to this latter, but in another key.[45]

'. . . that all the phrases of the melody of a Subject, which belong to the chord or to the key of the Tonic, should be repeated in the response, in similar phrases, belonging to the chord or to the key of the Dominant; and that all the phrases of a Subject, which bear analogy to the chord of the Dominant, should be repeated in the Response, in similar phrases, bearing analogy to the chord of the Tonic.'[46]

Added together, these rules combine to put subject and answer into a harmonic strait-jacket, in that they preclude the possibility of such situations as:

An answer to a non-modulating subject maintaining tonic tonality part-way through its course.

Answers to both modulating and non-modulating subjects maintaining tonic tonality throughout their respective courses.

An answer to a modulating subject making the converse modulation back to tonic via the key of the subdominant.

Yet, as we shall see, the above formulae are quite commonplace in actual practice.

Thus, neither of the above rules has any foundation in practice; and it must be counted unfortunate that their reiteration by subsequent theorists has resulted in a deep-rooted misunderstanding of this particular aspect of fugal answer. The failure of certain theorists to acknowledge the many subtle tonal relationships open to subject and answer led in turn to a spate of unwarranted strictures on eighteenth-century practice, with Bach the main target. Such phrases as 'I have in some instances criticized his [Bach's] procedure as regards the Answer'[47] became almost a commonplace in certain late nineteenth and early-twentieth century textbooks on fugue. Discussion of this point is renewed in the next chapter, but it should be pointed out that this practice was nothing new; for as early as the first quarter of the nineteenth century we see Fétis condemn an answer by Bach (Book II, No. XIII), and one by Pachelbel. He 'corrects' both answers from the standpoint of his own theories, but not before passing a severe, but undeserved stricture on the hapless Pachelbel: 'But what is not conceivable is Pachelbel's answer. . . . A fugue which is treated in this manner is merely a fantasy, a caprice; it is nothing, unless a genius such as that of John Sebastian Bach makes up for these shortcomings with beauties of a different kind.'[48]

Theory and practice thus part company, in that the earlier *conscious* distinction that was drawn between 'students' ' and 'composers' ' fugue is now, apparently, lost sight of.

---

[43] p. 67.
[44] p. 90.
[45] p. 63.
[46] p. 67.
[47] Kitson, *Fugal Construction*, Preface.
[48] J. F. Fétis, *Traité du contrepoint et de la fugue*, New ed. Paris, 1846, p. 42, para. 247. (First pub. Paris, 1824.)

CHAPTER II

PRACTICE AND THEORY

It has already been suggested that certain nineteenth- and twentieth-century theorists erroneously assumed that the decline of the old modal system saw a similar decline in the use of tonal answer, in that the two went hand in hand; that the eighteenth-century composer, from Bach and Handel onwards, no longer felt the necessity of being bound by a rule that originated before the establishing of the tonal system of their day.

The error of this assumption will, it is hoped, be made apparent as the chapter progresses, but sufficient at present to quote on this point from the theorists concerned. Prout writes: 'The old rule for fugal answer was that a subject made in either half of the authentic scale should be answered in the corresponding half of the plagal scale, and *vice versa*. For instance, if the subject began with the leap between tonic and dominant, in the lower half of the authentic scale, the answer would begin with the leap between dominant and tonic . . . This is a good rule enough, if it were only observed; but, as we shall proceed to show, the great masters, from Bach and Handel downwards, "drive a coach and four through it" continually.'[1] Later in the same chapter, in making a case for the alleged breaking of the 'old rule', Prout concludes, 'and it is quite evident that in many cases the great composers felt this to be of much more importance than the keeping of an old rule which was made before modern tonality was established.'[2]

Macpherson not only keeps this same theory alive, but goes one step further in his suggestion of inconsistency of application: 'The actual practice of the best fugal writers [in the use of tonal answer] differs so widely in numberless cases that it seems impossible to lay down actual rules for the answering of fugue-subjects beyond those which are virtually comprised in the statements just made.'[3] Macpherson is later joined by Kitson, when he complains of Bach's showing 'no consistency in the matter'.[4]

From statements such as these, it is clear that certain nineteenth- and twentieth-century theorists did not fully appreciate the principle of tonal answer as applied in practice by the eighteenth-century composer.

Failure to understand a period's procedure is one thing, but to try to force a composer's ideas into the mould of a preconceived theory is surely quite another. Theory overreached itself with a spate of unwarranted strictures such as that by Macpherson on Bach. Discussing Bach's answer to the subject of the *Musical Offering*, Macpherson writes: 'It was stated . . . that a Tonal reply is sometimes given to a subject which moves from Tonic to Dominant through the 3rd of the scale . . . but, with all respect to Bach, one has the instinctive feeling that the G marked X in the subject would have been better answered by D instead of C . . .'[5] And later, 'A similar criticism might be made in the case of the next example.'[6] (Bach, *Four Duets*, No. 2 in F—Ex. 76, p. 65.)

At another time, we find these same two theorists (Macpherson and Kitson) failing to agree among themselves. Commenting on the same example (Book I, No. 17),

---

[1] *Fugue*, pp. 32–33, paras. 85–86.
[2] p. 46, para. 108.
[3] S. Macpherson, *Studies in the Art of Counterpoint*, London, 1927, p. 99.
[4] *Fugal Construction*, p. 18.
[5] *Counterpoint*, p. 102.
[6] p. 102.

Macpherson finds that 'Bach... adheres to the old rule [of tonal answer] very effectively...'[7] Kitson on the other hand feels that this same answer 'to be consistent . . . should have been real'.[8] Premissing that Bach cannot be both right and wrong at the same time, it can only be inferred that one or the other of his critics lacks genuine insight into the period's technique. In a later chapter of this work,[9] I will attempt to prove that in this particular instance it is Kitson whose criticism is misplaced. Even so, Macpherson comes out little better, in that he omits to reason why, in two subjects whose openings are similarly constructed (both moving through the notes of the tonic chord), he approves of Bach's answer to the one, but not the other.

1. THE SIXTEENTH CENTURY

The inference to be drawn from Macpherson's criticism of the answer in the *Musical Offering* is that he regards a real answer under such circumstances as the more correct, and the more musical course.[10] An inference that could be drawn from his appraisal of Bach's behaviour in Book I, No. 17, is that in this particular case, Bach manages to 'get away with it' musically, in spite of the 'old rule'. From his general remarks on the tonal answer, it might further be inferred, that by Bach's time, the 'old rule' had had its day, anyway. Paradoxically, in disagreeing with Macpherson over this same subject (Book I, No. 17) Kitson is in effect lending his support to Macpherson's theory, which is that real, and not tonal answers should be given to subjects that commence with the arpeggio of the tonic chord.

This chapter attempts to prove that their theories, together with those of Prout concerning the tonal answer, are both wrong, and historically inaccurate.

Prior to the publication of Alfred Mann's *Study of Fugue* (1958), the question of the period in which the tonal answer took shape and became pronounced a rule was dealt with by theorists in a somewhat vague and loose manner. Albrechtsberger, for example, makes only a broad reference to 'this very ancient rule',[11] and Macpherson is no less vague in describing it as the 'old rule'. As we have just seen, Prout is more definite in relating it to modal times.[12]

It is not improbable that Prout's notion was fostered, at least in part, by the eighteenth-century theorist Johann Joseph Fux, who tells us in his famous *Gradus* that he has turned to Palestrina for his model. And so at this point we take in his explanation of the tonal answer from the section on fugue. His text is presented in the classical form of dialogue, such as Morley uses in his *Plaine and Easie Introduction*, and is allotted to the Master (Aloysius) and Pupil (Josephus).

In approaching Fux's *Gradus* two important considerations should be taken into account (i) his own admission of his indebtedness to Palestrina: 'Finally, for the sake of better understanding and greater clarity, I have used the form of dialogue. By *Aloysius*, the master, I refer to Palestrina, the celebrated light of music . . . to whom I owe every-thing that I know of this art',[13] and (ii) the influence of Palestrina upon his own style in *Gradus*, which was a return to the modal system:

---

[7] p. 103.
[8] *Fugal Construction*, p. 18.
[9] Chapter III 4. 'Subjects that open with notes of the Tonic Chord'.
[10] The same inference may be drawn from his remark 'In many cases where the subject begins with the "arpeggio" of the Tonic chord, both Bach and other fugal writers adopt the more musical course of answering Tonic harmony by Dominant *harmony*.' (*Counterpoint*, p. 102.)
[11] J. G. Albrechtsberger, *Gründliche Anweisung zur Composition*, trans. A. Merrick, London, 1844, Vol. I, p. 202.
[12] see p. 15.
[13] J. J. Fux, *Gradus ad Parnassum*, trans. and ed. A. Mann, London, 1944, p. 16.

Josephus: It seems to me that the diatonic system offers too few and inadequate possibilities and therefore leads necessarily to poor invention.

Aloysius: Doubtless it is more limited than the mixed system and does not open such a wide field for the imagination, but since it is best suited for learning the nature and characteristics of the modes, it becomes indispensable for acquiring the ability to write in a pure, unaccompanied style.[14]

Here, then, is Fux's discussion of the tonal answer:

Aloysius: A mode is further characterized by the fourth and fifth which make up its octave. According to the limits of these intervals, fugal themes will have to be arranged.

Ex. 10.   FUX, FROM GRADUS AD PARNASSUM

If the first part uses the skip of a fifth, the following part must use the skip of a fourth, in order not to exceed the limits of the mode or octave, and vice versa.[15]

Ex. 11.   IBID.

It is understandable that unless a person had studied Palestrina's music at first hand, he could quite easily be misled into accepting Fux's inflexible rule on the tonal answer as authoritative. It is by no means improbable therefore, that Prout's study of Fux, which he acknowledges in the Preface to his *Fugue*, plus his limited appreciation of modal times' music,[16] led him to the belief that the 'old rule' as he terms it, was pronounced before modern tonality was established. In view of the long unchallenged reign of his *Fugue* as the standard textbook on the subject, it is understandable perhaps that many of us at some time or other accepted his statement without question as being correct. The true facts of the case are very different.

As we saw in the previous chapter, with the exception of Vicentino, whose rule on the tonal answer concerned itself solely with fugue by inversion, none of the other great theorists, Ramos de Pareja, Zarlino, or Morley, pronounced any hard and fast rule on the matter. Indeed, we have to wait for the early Baroque to see a really positive pronouncement of the rule of tonal answer, and from then on it was seldom absent from contemporary theory. So that, far from being made 'before modern tonality was established', and falling into disuse with the disappearance of the modal system, it was the tonal period that persisted in its pronouncement in theory, and as we shall see, in its stricter application in practice. These facts show that Prout is inaccurate, and indicate that his approach to this particular aspect of tonal answer is basically unsound. So much for theory. What of sixteenth-century practice?

---

[14] J. J. Fux, *Gradus ad Parnassum, The Musical Quarterly,* XXXVI (1950), p. 539.
[15] p. 530.
[16] 'The first point to be considered in writing a fugue subject is *clear tonality* . . . . It is quite true that in many of the older fugues the tonality sounds vague and undecided; but this is because they were written in the old church modes, about which, except as a matter of antiquarian curiosity, the student need not trouble himself.' (*Fugue*, p. 6, para. 26.)

In order to arrive at a conclusive answer to this question, the 'exposition' sections of the following works were examined:

1. The Complete Works of Palestrina (Vols I–XXX)[17]
2. Works by Hugh Aston (1480–1522), Taverner, and Tallis.[18]
3. *The Collected Vocal Works of William Byrd.*[19]
4. The complete edition of *The English Madrigal School.*[20]

Examination of Palestrina's works revealed a substantial numerical superiority of *real* over *tonal* answers. This numerical superiority remains fairly constant throughout his creative life. This is stressed, in view of Lowinsky's claim that 'On the whole, the tonal answer occurs with increasing frequency in Palestrina's works, but the real answer by no means disappears.'[21] It is difficult to see how Lowinsky arrives at his conclusion, for although he is correct when he claims that the higher proportion of real over tonal answers in the motet book of 1563 is 'almost reversed in Palestrina's motet book of 1569',[22] this is not, as one might infer, a continuing trend. Indeed, it so happens that the proportion of tonal over real answers in the motet book of 1569[23] is greater than that of most other volumes. What is more, the greater number of volumes exhibits a larger proportion of real answers.

We return here to discuss more fully Jeppeson's references in his *Counterpoint* to the tonal answer. He writes, 'Tonal imitation was especially popular in the seventeenth and eighteenth centuries.' This, as we shall see, is true. He then goes on, 'In the sixteenth century, on the other hand, the real answer to a subject was preferred . . . one can, however, occasionally come upon tonal imitation...'[24] Although this latter claim is basically correct, we could be misled by the word 'occasionally', for it will have been gathered from the analysis given above, that preponderance of real over tonal answers notwithstanding, examples of tonal answers are not as rare as his paragraph would suggest. For example, in volume V alone of the complete works of Palestrina, we find seven examples of tonally answered 'subjects'. In another aspect, Jeppeson's summary is too broad a generalization; for the practice of the sixteenth-century English School differs quite considerably from that of the Roman School, in that it exhibits a marked preference for tonal over real answers. Byrd, for example, gives approximately three times as many tonal as real answers, and the English Madrigalists almost twice as many tonal as real answers. Their manneristic openings, such as Ex. 12a, more frequently than not are answered tonally somewhat as in Ex. 12b.

Ex. 12A. WARD, MADRIGAL, MY TRUE LOVE HATH MY HEART

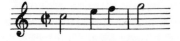

Ex. 12B. IBID.

The works of the earlier English composers, Aston, Tallis, and Taverner, on the other hand, show no marked preference for either tonal or real answers.

[17] *Le Opere Complete di Giovanni Pierluigi da Palestrina*, Rome, 1939–
[18] *Tudor Church Music*, London, 1922—vols. I, VI, X.
[19] *The Collected Vocal Works of William Byrd*, ed. E. H. Fellowes, London, 1937–
[20] *The English Madrigal School*, ed. E. H. Fellowes, London, 1921–
[21] *Tonality and Atonality*, p. 31.
[22] p. 31.
[23] Vol. V, *Motets for 5, 6, and 7 Voices*.
[24] *Counterpoint*, pp. 163–4.

We cannot dismiss these findings without discussing their possible significance. It has already been suggested (p. 5) that a stricter application of the tonal answer in the Baroque coincided with the establishment of our modern major-minor tonality. It was also suggested that our modern tonality manifested itself earlier in the sixteenth-century English School than in the Roman School of the same period. One has only to glance at such works as Wilbye's *Draw on Sweet Night*, Bateson's *If Love be Blind*, and Weelkes's *Our Country Swains*, to see the truth of this. And Morley's mind was firmly made up on the matter:

Philomathes: Have you no general rule to be given for an instruction for keeping of the key?

Master: No, for it must proceed only of the judgement of the composer; yet the churchmen for keeping their keys have devised certain notes commonly called the Eight Tunes . . . And these be, although not the true substance, yet some shadow of the ancient 'modi' whereof Boethius and Glareanus have written so much.

Phi.: I pray you set down those eight tunes, for the ancient 'modi' I mean by the grace of God to study hereafter.[25]

The significant factor uncovered by this survey, it is suggested, is that the English composer of this period, whose music clearly foreshadowed our modern tonality, apparently felt a more urgent need for definition of *key*, through the device of tonal answer, than did Palestrina, whose harmonic style was still more nearly related to the modal system. And it is not without significance that the later Englishmen used the tonal answer with greater regularity than did the earlier Aston, Tallis, and Taverner.

Summarizing the varying degrees of consistency in the use of tonal answer, we may say that the English stand midway between its more occasional application by Palestrina, and its relatively strict application by the seventeenth and eighteenth centuries. (The term 'relatively strict' will be discussed later.)

It is hoped that sufficient evidence has been advanced to demonstrate conclusively that Fux could not possibly have deduced his rule on the tonal answer from Palestrina's music; and that although originating as a *procedure* in the Renaissance, consistency of application, which after all is the justification for all rules, is not yet in evidence. For that we have to wait until the Baroque. Once this is accepted, it follows that in discussing the tonal answer in terms of Baroque practice, whether it be in Buxtehude or in Bach, it is incorrect chronologically to refer to it as 'the old rule', for it was not the Renaissance but the Baroque that pronounced it a rule, and, more important still, integrated it within its tonal system.

It remains to discuss one type of tonal answer which separates Renaissance from Baroque practice. A practice peculiar to the Renaissance is to open a work with a tonal answer *out of mode*;[26] that is, with cross-answering notes which define a mode different from that in which the work is written. Thus, Palestrina opens the motet *Cum pervenisset beatus Andreas* in a manner suggestive of the Ionian mode (Ex. 13a), whereas the ending of the composition (Ex. 13b) declares the mode to be Mixolydian:

---

[25] *Plaine and Easie Introduction*, p. 249.
[26] A survival of this custom is to be seen in certain of Pachelbel's ninety-four *Interludes to the Magnificat*, which were composed for each of the eight tones.

c

Ex. 13A.   Palestrina, Motet, Cum pervenisset beatus Andreas

Ex. 13B.   ibid.

A further example is seen in his madrigal *Ovver de' sensi è priva* where the opening suggests Dorian (Ex. 14a), but which finally declares itself Aeolian. (Ex. 14b):

Ex. 14A.   Palestrina, Madrigal, Ovver de' sensi è priva

Ex. 14B.   ibid.

It is quite possible that the subjects in Ex. 15a and 15b are a survival of this practice.

Ex. 15A.   J. S. Bach, 'Forty-Eight', Book II, No. 5

Ex. 15B.   Handel, Clavier Fugue in B minor

Unlike the Palestrina examples above, however, neither subject is answered tonally; moreover, even this form of opening is not now generally accepted, for on these two same subjects Marpurg comments: 'The leap from the octave of the main key to the lower fifth was forbidden according to the rules of the old masters because it rendered uncertain the establishment of the key.'[27]

---

[27] *Abhandlung*, Part I, Chap. III, Section 1, p. 26. (Notes to Tab. XII, figs. 1 and 2.)

2. THE SEVENTEENTH AND EIGHTEENTH CENTURIES

It has been pointed out, that whereas none of the great Renaissance theorists whose work we have discussed laid down rules for the tonal answer (discounting Vicentino's rule concerning fugue in contrary motion), from the seventeenth century onwards few if any writers on fugue omitted to do so. The cardinal error of certain nineteenth-century theorists was their assumption that in times earlier than Bach and Handel, the rule of tonal answer was regarded as absolute. Prout in such a phrase as 'A further proof that but little weight was attached to the necessity for a tonal answer'[28] implies an attitude of casual indifference on the part of the Baroque composer. The true fact of the case is that the rule never was regarded as absolute, either in theory, or in practice. Proof of this is not difficult to produce. Fortunately for us, a number of earlier writers on fugue were not only theorists, but composers as well; or more accurately put, composer-theorists. Purcell declares unequivocally his own attitude towards rules in general: 'The first Thing to treat of is *Counterpoint*, and in this I must differ from Mr *Simpson*, (whose *Compendium* I admire as the most Ingenious Book I e're met with upon this Subject;) but his Rule in Three Parts for *Counterpoint* is too strict, and destructive to good Air, which ought to be preferr'd before such Nice Rules.'[29] As we have already seen, and shall see again, instances are not wanting in his own compositions where 'good Air is preferr'd before Nice Rules'. Only a cynic would declare his a tongue-in-cheek attitude. Fux's unbending rule notwithstanding, he himself can write:

Ex. 16. Fux, Missa Purificationis

We have already seen Rameau deliberately going out of his way to demonstrate that the rule of tonal answer was by no means absolute, and like Purcell before him, reminding us that music cannot be reduced to fixed rules.[30] Marpurg, admittedly a theorist first and foremost, gives as a matter of course a whole group of irregularly answered subjects in his *Abhandlung von der Fuge*. Exceptions to his own rule are by no means difficult to find in Albrechtsberger's compositions:

Ex. 17A. Albrechtsberger, Fugue in D minor

Ex. 17B. Albrechtsberger, Fugue in C

And as we earlier remarked (p. 14), in one instance Cherubini was compelled to admit, his 'immutable rule' notwithstanding, that a tonal answer could not be permitted to stand in the way of other and more important musical considerations.

---

[28] *Fugue*, p. 46, para. 109.
[29] Playford, *Art of Descant*, p. 105.
[30] See pp. 7-8.

This, then, is perhaps the best place to discuss the whole principle of tonal answer as understood by the Baroque. The conclusions drawn are based upon an extensive examination of a wide circle of composers extending fully over, and indeed far beyond the Baroque period:

Johann Kaspar Kerll	(1627–1693).	D. Buxtehude	(1637–1707).
J. P. Krieger	(1649–1725).	J. Pachelbel	(1653–1706).
V. Lübeck	(1656–1740).	J. Kuhnau	(1660–1722).
H. Purcell	(1658–1695).	J. S. Bach	(1685–1750).
J. G. Walther	(1684–1748).	T. Roseingrave	(1690–1766).
G. F. Handel	(1685–1759).	J. Eberlin	(1702–1762).
Gottlieb Muffat	(1690–1770).	J. G. Albrechtsberger	(1736–1809).
J. Keeble	(1711–1786).	C. F. G. Schwenke	(1767–1822).
J. H. Knecht	(1752–1817).		

The inclusion of certain less-known composers is deliberate.

This examination revealed a remarkably consistent degree of behaviour in these composers' attitude towards the tonal answer. It may be claimed that far from displaying an attitude of casual indifference, their work shows that they regarded the tonal answer as a relatively strict procedure. By 'relatively strict' is meant, that apart from deference to certain overriding musical considerations, such as Ex. 7 from Purcell, in the overwhelming majority of cases a tonal answer would be given when called for. Certain firm basic principles may be deduced from Baroque practice:

When appropriate, and provided both harmonic and melodic conditions permitted, a tonal answer would normally be given.

Even though apparently appropriate, the claim of tonal answer never overruled that of spontaneous musical impulse. For example, should the answer's point of entry coincide with a modulation, its form (tonal or real) would be determined by the harmony.

It will be shown that it is this, the subordination of melody to the stronger claim of harmony, that accounts for the majority of so-called 'irregular' answers. Here we are reminded of Schumann's aphorism: 'Music resembles chess. The queen (melody) has the greatest power, but the king (harmony) decides the game.' Indeed, it might well have been written as a terse summary of the above points, for it contains the very essence of the Baroque's attitude towards tonal versus real answer. We need only modify Kurth's observation relating to Palestrina's practice on p. 80, by deleting the words 'more and more' and 'especially of the middle parts', and the picture is in full perspective.

The tonal design of a movement or of a whole work would sometimes exercise its influence over the form of an answer.[31]

A real answer in preference to a tonal one would also be given, should the latter result in an ungainly melodic line.

But it is again stressed, that far from being a matter of casual indifference, from the seventeenth century onwards, the tonal answer became an integral part of fugal technique.

Before discussing these principles in detail let us first review briefly seven from the given list of composers, whose creative years span the greater part of the Baroque period.

Buxtehude. In his organ *Preludes and Fugues*,[32] every one of the twenty-six subjects inviting tonal answers is satisfied. Furthermore, every one of his subjects commencing on the dominant note is answered either tonally or subdominantly throughout.

---

[31] The real answer to the subject of the fugue that concludes the E minor Clavier Toccata (Ex. 118a) and the unusally answered subject of the final fugue of Handel's *Dixit Dominus* (Ex. 172a) are two cases in point. They are discussed in Chapters V and VII respectively.
[32] *Complete Organ Works*, Vol. II (Novello).

J. P. Krieger. Some seventy-five fugues were examined. Of thirty-one subjects inviting tonal answers, all but four are given one. All twenty-six fugues commencing on the dominant note are given either a tonal answer, or a subdominant one.

Lübeck. In his six organ *Preludes and Fugues*, all ten situations inviting tonal answers are satisfied.

Purcell. The *Twelve Sonatas of Three Parts*, and the *Ten Sonatas of Four Parts* were chosen as representative of his fugal style. Of seventeen similar situations in the *Ten Sonatas of Four Parts*, eleven subjects are either answered tonally, or given a subdominant response; and of some sixteen similar situations in the *Twelve Sonatas of Three Parts*, eleven subjects are either answered tonally or given a subdominant response.

Pachelbel. Ninety-four *Interludes to the Magnificat*. Of the forty-one fugue subjects inviting tonal response, all but eight are satisfied. Of the forty-six subjects that open on the dominant, all but two are either answered tonally, or given a subdominant response.

Gottlieb Muffat. (*Denkmäler der Tonkunst in Österreich*—Band 58.) Of the thirty-six fugues with subjects inviting tonal response, all but two are satisfied. All twenty-four fugues that open on the dominant are either answered tonally, or given a subdominant response.

J. S. Bach. Of some one hundred and sixty subjects found inviting tonal answers all but a score or so are satisfied. In the 'Forty-Eight' alone for example, of the thirty subjects inviting some form of tonal response, all but three are given it. And as we shall see, the three subjects that are not answered tonally belong to a particular melodic structure that is very rarely given other than a real answer.[33]

In themselves these statistics are weighty enough, but in order to convince thoroughly, our task must be one of accounting satisfactorily for the relatively small group of *real* answers given to subjects inviting *tonal* response. From this examination it was concluded that almost invariably so-called exceptions to the rule were the result of one or the other of the situations outlined on p. 22.

Examples of real answers, the result of harmonic circumstance.

Ex. 18. Purcell, Ten Sonatas of Four Parts, No. 10

Ex. 18 provides a good example of an answer taking its form from the harmony. The opening leap from tonic to dominant would normally call for a tonal answer, but the move to the dominant key precludes this possibility. The cadential harmonies are thus the determining factor. Similar situations are quite plentiful: for example, the 'subjects' in Nos. 2 (*Andante*), 6 (*Canzona*), 8 (*Allegro*), and 10 (*Presto*) of *Twelve Sonatas of Three Parts* by Purcell, and in Nos. 2 (*Allegro*), 6 (*Largo*), 7 (*Allegro*), and 12 (*Allegro*) of *Sonata de chiesa*, Op. 1 by Corelli are all given real, in place of expected tonal, answers. As in Ex. 18, they take their form from the cadential harmonies—frequently V-I in the key of the dominant. In Ex. 19, the resultant harmonic situation at X would also preclude the possibility of a tonal answer.[34]

[33] See pp. 38–43, and Exx. 41–44.
[34] This claim will be investigated in the next chapter, but see also pp. 26–27 and Exx. 25-28.

Ex. 19.   PURCELL, TEN SONATAS OF FOUR PARTS, No. 5

The next two examples from *Messiah* illustrate the same point admirably, in that their respective openings are somewhat alike:

Ex. 20A.   HANDEL, MESSIAH

Ex. 20B.   IBID.

The ending of the subject of Ex.20a moves easily into a tonal answer, but in Ex. 20b the modulation to the dominant key precludes possibility of tonal reply. As with Ex. 18, the answer's form is determined by the harmony. One would normally expect Ex. 21a to be answered as in Ex. 21b:

Ex. 21A.   J. S. BACH, CLAVIER TOCCATA IN D MINOR

Ex. 21B.

But a modulation to A minor is effected before the entry of the answer, hence the **real** reply, which grows naturally out of the cadential harmonies:

Ex. 21c.   IBID.

It may be recalled (p. 13) that Marpurg strongly condemned procedure of this kind as 'a fundamental error at the beginning of a fugue, and only allowed those so-called fashionable (galant) composers who permit themselves to write something whereof they can give not just cause'.

Exx. 22 and 23 from Bach explain themselves. The effect of a tonal answer on the melodic line of Ex. 22 might also be taken into account.

Ex. 22.   J. S. BACH, ORGAN FANTASIA AND FUGUE IN A MINOR

Ex. 23.   J. S. BACH, CLAVIER FUGUE IN D MINOR

The reason for the real answer in Ex. 24 from Pachelbel lies in the construction of the movement, which is sometimes termed a 'close' fugue.[35] The opening notes of the answer must perforce grow out of the cadential harmonies at the point of overlap between subject and answer.

Ex. 24.   PACHELBEL, INTERLUDES TO THE MAGNIFICAT, V. 12

[35] 'One in which the Answer follows the Subject—overlaps in *Stretto* style—from the beginning.' R. Dunstan, *A Cyclopaedic Dictionary of Music*, 4th ed., London, 1925, p. 198.

In Exx. 25 and 26, a tonal reply would involve using the bare tritone—a procedure beyond the harmonic technique of Purcell's day.[36]

Ex. 25. PURCELL, TWELVE SONATAS OF THREE PARTS, NO. 12

Ex. 26. PURCELL, TEN SONATAS OF FOUR PARTS, NO. 7

A tonal answer in Ex. 27 would involve the upper voice in a leap to the diminished fifth of the bare tritone.

Ex. 27. J. S. BACH, CLAVIER FUGUE IN B FLAT

[36] The Gigue from Bach's fifth *English Suite* and Book II No. 13 in F sharp major provide rare examples of this. A fugue by Johann Bernhard Bach (1676-1749) contained in K. Geiringer's collection, *Music of the Bach Family* (Cambridge, Mass., 1955, p. 74), is the only other instance of its use that I have come across.

Even Knecht, who chronologically belongs to the Classical era, solves the same problem in like manner:

Ex. 28.   KNECHT, CLAVIER FUGUE IN D

The final example in this group (Ex. 29) is one of Pachelbel's *Interludes to the Magnificat*. It is quoted in full, because it provides an exceptionally lucid illustration of the give and take between the rival claims of tonal answer and harmony. Its form is that of a double fugue, the two subjects ultimately combining:

Ex. 29.   PACHELBEL, INTERLUDES TO THE MAGNIFICAT, VIII. 8

29

Fugue I. The subject, which commences on the dominant, is answered tonally in bars three and nine. The harmonic factor determines the answer's real form at its next entry in bar twenty-three, but permits a further tonal answer in bar twenty-eight.

Fugue II. The double bar initiates a fugue on a new subject, and as in Fugue I, the first two answers are tonal. (Bars forty-two and forty-six.) A tonal answer at bar fifty-one would have resulted in VII_4^6—clearly beyond the period's technique. The harmony again stands in the way of a tonal answer in bar fifty-six, but permits one in bar sixty. The two subjects combine in bar sixty-six, and throughout this part of the fugue a tonal answer is given only when the various harmonic situations permit. (See Subject I in bars sixty-six, eighty-three, eighty-five, and ninety.) In all other cases (Subject I in bar seventy-two and Subject II in bars sixty-six, seventy-two, and eighty-six), real answers are given, taking their form from prevailing harmonic conditions.

Real answers, the result of melodic line. A second cause which may at times be held to account for so-called 'irregular' answers, arises when a tonal reply threatens to result in an ungainly melodic line. Several theorists including Prout, A. W. Marchant, and Macpherson, have attributed certain irregular answers to this cause. It is upon this issue, of what does and what does not constitute an awkward melodic line, that composers and theorists tend to disagree. Such an issue must remain a personal one, surely, for the individual composer's judgement. The theorist's view must always be a subjective one. Lovelock, for example, condemns the answer in Ex. 30 as 'unmusical on account of the major 7th G to F sharp being taken in two leaps'.[37]

Ex. 30. LOVELOCK, FROM THE EXAMINATION FUGUE

Yet Bach can write:

---

[37] W. Lovelock, *The Examination Fugue*, London, p. 43. Even so, Marpurg, in discussing Ex. 31b from Fux, is at pains to justify this very melodic shape! (*Abhandlung*, Part I, Chap. III, Sec. 11, p. 59.)

Ex. 31A. J. S. Bach, French Suite, No. 5

and Fux:

Ex. 31B. Fux, from Marpurg's Abhandlung von der Fuge

and Pachelbel:

Ex. 31C. Pachelbel, Interludes to the Magnificat, II. 6

Again, Bairstow, in discussing the tonal answer writes: 'These note changes are not arbitrary. In some cases they give variety and character to the answer; in others they spoil the contour. The latter is often the case when the notes of the tonic triad succeed each other. Ex. [32a] would never be answered as at [32b].'[38]

Ex. 32A. Bairstow, from Counterpoint and Harmony

Ex. 32B. ibid.

Yet we see Bach answering a subject precisely thus:

Ex. 33. J. S. Bach, Cantata No. 21, Ich hatte viel Bekümmernis

Or take Prout's criticism of Handel—'adherence to the old rule will sometimes injure the form of the answer. This will be seen in the following example:'

[38] E. C. Bairstow, *Counterpoint and Harmony*, London, 1937, p. 320.

33

Ex. 34A.   HANDEL, HERCULES

'Here the character of the subject is entirely ruined by the monotonous repetition of the F's in the answer. A real answer here would have been far more effective.'[39]

Such procedure is not uncommon in Handel, as Ex. 34b and 34c show:

Ex. 34B.   HANDEL, CLAVIER SUITE, NO. 2 IN F

Ex. 34C.   HANDEL, CLAVIER SUITE, NO. 6 IN F SHARP MINOR

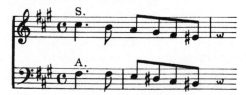

It is bold criticism on Prout's part, for similarly answered subjects, which are not difficult to find, prove Handel to be in excellent company:

Ex. 35A.   RIGHINI, FROM A. W. MARCHANT'S FUGUE SUBJECTS AND ANSWERS

Ex. 35B.   W. F. BACH, FROM A. W. MARCHANT'S FUGUE SUBJECTS AND ANSWERS

[39] *Fugue*, p. 40, para. 100.

Ex. 35c.   J. S. Bach, The Art of Fugue, Contrapunctus XIX

Ex. 35d.   Telemann, from A. W. Marchant's Fugue Subjects and Answers

Ex. 35e.   W. F. Bach, Durch Adams Fall ist ganz verderbt

And how many of us would, with confidence, contract the octave into a seventh for the sake of answering the subject in Ex. 36 tonally?

Ex. 36.   Roseingrave, Fugue in B flat

Yet this is precisely what Roseingrave does! Arthur Hutchings stresses the same point—'*If mutation is awkward, do not hesitate to use a subdominant answer. . . .* This example [Book I, No. 18] is from one of the only two fugues in the "Forty Eight" that have a modulating subject in the minor key. Such subjects usually cause ungainliness when we attempt an answer by mutation. . . . I have searched in vain for a specimen devised by a French theorist and said to include three different notes which are "correctly" answered by three soundings of the same note.'[40]

The subject of Arthur Hutchings's fruitless search no doubt is either Ex. 37a–37c from André Gédalge's *Traité de la fugue*,[41] or Ex. 38a–38b from Charles Koechlin's *Etude sur l'écriture de la fugue d'école*.[42]

[40] *Invention and Composition*, pp. 90–91.
[41] A. Gédalge, *Traité de la fugue*, Paris, 1901, pp. 22–23, paras. 46–48, and pp. 50–55, paras. 92–98.
[42] C. Koechlin, *Etude sur l'écriture de la fugue d'école*, Paris, 1933, p. 7 and pp. 136–8.

D

Ex. 37B. ibid.

Ex. 37C. ibid.

Ex. 38A. Koechlin, from Etude sur l'écriture de la fugue d'école

Ex. 38B. ibid.

We are fairly safe in assuming that Tovey is referring to Koechlin's answer (Ex. 38a) when he writes: 'there are numerous cases where it is said to be difficult to find a correct answer. The recent very learned treatise on *La Fugue d'Ecole* makes out an excellent and honest case for the admittedly fictitious scholastic fugue as a discipline, but in my opinion demolishes its case completely by gravely demonstrating that for a certain subject beginning with three adjacent notes the only correct answer is one of three identical notes, whether the fugue be scholastic or genuinely musical. The rules which make such a case difficult ought to be swept into limbo. Three identical notes are on no conceivable ruling an answer to a subject of three different notes.'[43]

So far as fugal answer is concerned, the making of positive statements such as this can be dangerous in that they are liable to rebound. Consider for example the following subject and answer by Thomas Attwood:

EX. 39.   ATTWOOD, FROM THEORIE- UND KOMPOSITIONSSTUDIEN BEI MOZART

The main interest of this particular subject and answer lies not in the exactness of their outlines to those of Gédalge and Koechlin, but in the fact that the fugue from which they are taken was written by Attwood under Mozart's personal supervision. That Mozart was satisfied with Attwood's answer is substantiated by the direct evidence contained in the liberal corrections in Mozart's own hand during the ensuing part of the fugue.[44]   And even though this particular answer may appear somewhat stiff, is it so very different from the answer which Mozart himself gives in Ex. 145 on p. 156 (whose threefold sounding of D in answer to three different notes is also a consequence of tonal answer), or from those by W. F. Bach and Telemann quoted in Ex. 35d and 35e?

The rather unusual form of the answers in Exx. 37 and 38 may be accounted for in part by the fact that in devising them, Gédalge and Koechlin had in mind the rule which forbids the answer to move in a direction contrary to that of the subject. (See p. 182.)   This rule as given by another writer, E. J. Dent, reads: 'If the subject moves downwards, the answer must either do the same or stand still on the same note; it must not under any circumstances move upwards.'   He 'proves' the rule thus:

'if the subject has
| soh: soh, fah | me, ray: doh |
the tonal answer will be
| doh': doh', doh' | te, lah: soh |
and *not*
| doh': ray', doh' | te, lah: soh |

as we might well be tempted to write, thinking it more musical.   It probably is; but it infringes the strict rule that the answer must never move in a direction contrary to that shown in the subject.'[45]

Yet Johann Friedrich Fasch had no compunction in flouting the rule in his B flat Sonata for flute, oboe, violin and continuo:

EX. 40   J. F. FASCH, SONATA FOR FLUTE OBOE VIOLIN AND CONTINUO IN B FLAT

[43] *Musical Textures*, pp. 25–26.
[44] Attwood, *Kompositionsstudien*, p. 162.
[45] E. J. Dent, *Notes on Fugue for Beginners*, Cambridge, 1958, p. 23.

According to both Gédalge and Dent, his answer, to be correct, should have opened with a four-fold sounding of the initial B flat, and should not in any circumstances have moved upwards to the D.

The plain fact is, you can never be absolutely certain where you are when it comes to an answer's shape.

But it is when we come across a subject with a distinctive melodic pattern receiving, more often than not, a real rather than an expected tonal answer, that we may be fairly certain that considerations of character and shape are involved.

Such a subject, with alternative answers by Rameau has already been quoted. (Ex. 5a and 5b, p. 8.) It will be recalled that Rameau's solution was either a real answer or a partially subdominant one. The melodic structure of this subject's opening is a move from tonic to supertonic, followed by a direct downward skip to dominant. Tonic and dominant notes are thus in relatively close proximity. It is significant that real answers are consistently applied to the group of similarly constructed subjects[46] in Ex. 41a–41o.

Ex. 41A.   J. S. BACH, ORGAN PRELUDE AND FUGUE IN A MINOR

Ex. 41B.   ZACHOW, CANTATA, ES WIRD EINE RUTE AUFGEHEN

Ex. 41C.   J. L. KREBS, FROM A. W. MARCHANT'S FUGUE SUBJECTS AND ANSWERS

[46] There is a downward leap from supertonic to dominant in Exx. 142 (a) and 144, but in both these, mutation is effected by tonally answering the subject's seventh degree—a degree that is generally amenable to mutation.

Ex. 41D.   J. S. Bach, Clavier Fugue in D minor

Ex. 41E.   J. S. Bach, Organ Sonata No. 6

Ex. 41F.   J. S. Bach, Organ Prelude and Fugue in C minor

Ex. 41G.   Albrechtsberger, Fugue in D minor

Ex. 41H. ZACHOW, CLAVIER PRELUDE AND FUGUE IN C

Ex. 41I. J. S. BACH, 'FORTY-EIGHT', BOOK II, No. 18

Ex. 41J. J. S. BACH, GOLDBERG VARIATIONS, No. 10

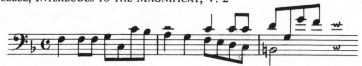

Ex. 41K. PACHELBEL, INTERLUDES TO THE MAGNIFICAT, V. 2

Ex. 41L. MOZART, CLAVIER FUGUE IN C MINOR, K.383

Ex. 41M. J. S. BACH, 'FORTY-EIGHT', BOOK I, No. 9

Ex. 41n. J. S. Bach, 'Forty-Eight', Book II, No. 4

Ex. 41o. Gottlieb Muffat, Clavier and Organ Fugue in B flat

The basic cause of the difficulty is the interposition of the supertonic between tonic and dominant. Unless mutation is effected at a point before the supertonic is reached, the inescapable consequence of replying tonally is that the original downward leap of a fifth must become stretched to a sixth. (I have yet to encounter an actual example of this in practice.)

However, assuming a tonal reply is given, either by dropping a sixth, or effecting mutation before the supertonic is reached, a further difficulty is that unless the subsequent melodic line permits a *second* mutation, the answer must complete itself at subdominant level, which is all very well if you really want it that way.

Ex. 42a. Purcell, Twelve Sonatas of Three Parts, No. 1

Ex. 42b. Purcell, Ten Sonatas of Four Parts, No. 4

In Ex. 42a and 42b we do indeed see Purcell in two similarly constructed subjects giving the same solution as Rameau's alternative (Ex. 5b), which, it will be recalled, is a partially subdominant answer. But to balance this, in Ex. 42a, the expedient of reversing the interval sequence at * (so that tone is answered by semitone, and minor by major third) arrests the flatward drift, guiding the tonality instead into the relative major; and in 42b the tonal answer becomes the means of restoring the tonic key following the modulation in the subject to the dominant. In short, in 42b, the answer necessarily had to follow a subdominant course in order to arrive back finally in the tonic. A parallel case to Ex. 42b is Ex. 142g (p. 153) from Kirnberger.

Thus, the reply to a modulating subject answering to this particular melodic pattern presents no problem. But with the reply to a non-modulating subject, which at some point needs to readjust to dominant level of reply, the case is different. Return to Ex. 41 (pp. 38–41), and experiment by attempting to reply tonally to any of the subjects in this group. Two possibilities present themselves:

(i) Effect mutation before the supertonic is reached, and attempt to regain dominant level once the dominant note has been replied to tonally.

(ii) Effect mutation immediately following the supertonic, so that the drop of the fifth becomes stretched to a sixth.

This latter solution immediately destroys a characteristic melodic motive. Even so, assuming mutation to be effected here, an attempt to gain dominant level of reply will succeed only at a cost; either certain of the subject's characteristic intervals will be eliminated, or the course of a diatonic or chromatic scale line interrupted, or the breaking up of a melodic sequence, or the substitution of an ungainly interval for what originally was a shapely one. Each of these can detract in one way or another from the gainliness or, expressed in another way, from the essential character of the melodic line.[47]

From the evidence of practice it would appear that the only reasonable solution to subjects answering to this particular melodic pattern, is either to give a real answer (as in Ex. 41a–41o), or to effect a two-fold mutation—one at the answer's outset, and a second one following the tonal reply. A particularly fascinating example of the latter course comes from Eberlin. Undaunted by the difficulties involved, and determined apparently to answer the subject's tonic and dominant notes tonally, Eberlin gains his point by exercising his ingenuity in a solution involving a two-fold mutation:

Ex. 43.—EBERLIN, CLAVIER FUGUE IN D MINOR

Bach applies this same solution in Book I, No. 23 (see Ex. 144, p. 155) but at a cost, for his answer, 'on which more ink has been spilt than if Bach had had twenty *wives*',[48] has excited comment, favourable and otherwise, ever since. A less familiar work of Bach's whose subject and answer are identical in shape to the first eight notes of subject and answer alike of Book I, No. 23 (but which, understandably, has escaped similar attention), is the fugue from his *Prelude, Fugue, and Allegro in E flat* for Lute or Clavier. (BWV 998.) (See Ex. 142a, p. 151.) In this same connection see also Ex. 142d (p. 152) from Schwenke.

[47] This need, to preserve characteristic intervals from subject to answer, is stressed for example by Marpurg in his analysis of the answer to the subject of Book I, No. 18: 'For this movement the Answer has been taken from the Fourth, whereas were it to have been in the Fifth, it would then have been organised in such a manner as is expressed within the figure [musical example] shown here.' (This shows mutation effected between the two notes forming the augmented fourth.) 'This however has not been done: (a) because the interval of the Tritone g–c sharp would then have had to be changed to the Third d–f sharp, and this change would have been more unusual than the change from the Second g–f sharp to the Third d–b natural: (b) because this alteration of the scales produces more harmony.' (*Abhandlung*, Part I, Chap. III, Section 3, p. 30 and Tab. XIV, Fig. 4.)
[48] A. E. F. Dickinson, *Bach's Fugal Works*, London, 1956, p. 166.

Both these answers are discussed in connection with a different aspect in Chap. VI.

No less fascinating is the young Thomas Attwood's answer to a similarly constructed subject:

Ex. 44. ATTWOOD, FROM THEORIE- UND KOMPOSITIONSSTUDIEN BEI MOZART

Although this was written during his period of study under Mozart, it is unfortunate that Attwood's notebook, from which this example is taken[49] affords no evidence as to his teacher's reaction to this answer. Even so, we should at least be grateful to him for demonstrating the very sort of situation that composers in general, apparently, were content to avoid.

The fact that there are relatively few exceptions (as in Exx. 42 (p. 41), 43 (p. 42), 142a (p. 151), 142d (p. 152) and 144 (p. 155)), lends support to the contention that this particular melodic shape was less amenable than most to tonal answer; and that unless the melodic line permitted a two-fold mutation (as in most of these exceptions) composers preferred to give a real answer rather than sacrifice distinctly characteristic features of the subject.

Consider the effect of a tonal answer upon the melodic line of Ex. 45:

Ex. 45. J. S. BACH, CLAVIER FANTASIA AND FUGHETTA IN B FLAT

Another melodic formation which if answered tonally would yield a questionable result, is seen in Ex. 46a and 46b.

Ex. 46A. DROBS, FUGUE IN A MINOR

Ex. 46B. PACHELBEL, CHORALE PRELUDE, ES SPRICHT DER UNWEISEN MUND WOHL

49 *Kompositionsstudien*, p. 269.

43

Answered tonally, Exx. 45, and 46a and 46b would produce respectively Ex. 47a, 47b, and 47c:

Ex. 47A.

Ex. 47B.

Ex. 47C.

Yet a further one is when the subject consists of an unbroken scalic run, from tonic up to dominant. (See pp. 11-12.)

To summarize this chapter:

The evidence of Baroque practice provides ample proof that composers themselves never did regard the so-called 'rule' of tonal answer as being inflexible. The Baroque did, however, regard the tonal answer as a relatively strict basic procedure; and subject to the overriding local claims of harmony and melodic line, in the vast majority of cases a tonal reply would be given when called for. The strictures of Prout and Macpherson notwithstanding, behaviour regarding the tonal answer was remarkably clear and consistent throughout the entire course of the Baroque.

We conclude Part I of this work by attempting to reconcile the opposed viewpoints[50] concerning the origin and purpose of tonal answer; of Prout and Oldroyd's on the one hand, who view its continuing use in the Baroque as nothing more than a lingering modal custom, and of Reese and Lowinsky's on the other, who link the increasing frequency of its use within the gradual growth of the tonal system.

From what has been said it would appear that theory and practice of the Renaissance and the Baroque combine to put the issue beyond doubt: the viewpoint of Reese and Lowinsky, that the widespread use of tonal answer goes hand in hand with the decline of the modal system and the gradual growth of the tonal system, is the correct one.

As far as theory is concerned, what has emerged is that whereas none of the great Renaissance writers pronounce any hard-and-fast rule on the tonal answer, the rule governing its use is seldom absent from Baroque theory. In turn, this is a reflection of the respective practices of the two periods; its rather more tentative appearance in the Renaissance, crystallizing in the early Baroque into what might fairly be termed a relatively strict procedure, in that it now becomes integrated within the period's tonal system.

Standing midway between the Roman school and the early Baroque is the sixteenth-century English School, whose more frequent use of the tonal answer than that of its Italian contemporary, Palestrina, goes hand-in-hand, significantly, with this School's earlier predilection for major-minor tonality.

At this point it may be pertinent to ask, if the device of tonal answer, as Prout and Oldroyd would have it, was integrated within the modal system, how was it that the widespread and increasing frequency of its use coincided simultaneously with the decline of that system, and the growing feeling for the newer major-minor tonality?

The purpose of the remaining chapters is a detailed investigation into modern fugal theory as it affects the answer, with special reference to the standard textbooks' approach.

[50] See Introduction.

PART II

CHAPTER III

TONAL ANSWER AND MODERN THEORY

1. PRELIMINARY—TONALITY OF SUBJECT AND ANSWER

Many theorists, including Cherubini, Higgs, Prout, Gédalge, Macpherson and others, describe the answer as a transposition of the subject into the *key* of the dominant. Macpherson's explanation is characteristic—'When the Subject is in the Tonic key . . . the Answer will be a transposition of that subject into the Dominant key. . .'[1]

Although this is sometimes the case, it is by no means as invariable as the rule would suggest.

It was said on p. 19 that the tonal answer became an integral part of Baroque fugal technique. This was not solely a matter of replying tonally to tonic and dominant. Were this the case, it could hardly be claimed as an essential part of fugal technique, for it would then amount to little more than respect for an erstwhile tradition. Almost invariably, the tonal answer is bound up with some particular aspect of tonality; the means of creating some subtle tonal relationship between subject and answer; of deferring modulation; of effecting tonal balance between a modulating subject and its answer. Each of these will be fully discussed in turn. For the moment, let us see the effect of three different types of tonal response on the tonal relationship between subject and answer.

In the 'Forty-Eight' six subjects open with a leap from tonic to dominant. They are Book I, Nos. 2, 8, 17, 22; and Book II, Nos. 7, 11. All six are replied to tonally. Furthermore, in all six, modulation to the dominant does not coincide with the commencement of the answer, as the textbook rule would have it. Instead, tonic tonality is maintained in varying degrees part-way through the answer, and in one instance (Book I, 17 in A flat) completely through it, so that subject and answer are bound by one common tonality. Another case of this, of subject and answer remaining in the tonic key throughout (rendered possible by the device of tonal answer), is Contrapunctus IV of *The Art of Fugue;* and, almost so, Concerto Grosso No. 11 of Op. 6 by Handel.

A further seven subjects have tonic and dominant notes in relatively close proximity. They are Book I, Nos. 9, 19, and 23; and Book II, Nos. 3, 4, 18, and 21. Of these, Nos. 19 and 23 of Book I, and Nos. 3 and 21 of Book II are given tonal answers. Again, in all four, tonic tonality is maintained part-way through their respective answers.

It is perhaps not without significance that the three subjects whose respective dominant notes are not replied to tonally (Book I, No. 9, and Book II, Nos. 4 and 18), all answer to the melodic structure discussed on pp. 38–43, and illustrated by examples 41a–41o, in which they are included.

In the 'Forty-Eight' seventeen subjects commence on the dominant. They are Book I, Nos. 3, 7, 11, 12, 13, 16, 21, and 24; and Book II, Nos. 1, 2, 12, 14, 15, 16, 17, 20, and 24. Again, all seventeen are answered tonally, and once more we see the effect of tonal reply upon the key relationship between subject and answer. See for example No. 11 in Book I, Nos. 1 and 21 in Book II, where tonic tonality is maintained well into the answer, and

---

[1] *Counterpoint*, p. 99.

No. 7 in Book I where the answer is in the tonic key throughout. In *attacco* subjects, such as Book I, Nos. 17 and 19, and Book II, No. 3, the motive is plain. A rigid alternation between tonic and dominant keys in short-breathed subjects such as these, would bring them dangerously close to the deliberately ludicrous situations in Mozart's *Ein Musikalischer Spass*.[2] Instead, resort to tonal answer opens the way for the exposition of No. 17 to remain predominantly in the key of the tonic, and for the exposition of No. 19 to afford a remarkable study in miniature of subtle tonal relationships between subject and answer.

Tovey is to the point concerning such examples as these, when he raises the question 'whether the alternation between subject and answer is an alternation between two keys, or an alternation between two positions of the same scale'.[3]

A third type of tonal answer is the free exchange between subject and answer of tones and semitones. Two cases of this are given in Exx. 48 and 49:

Ex. 48.   J. S. Bach, Clavier Fugue in C

Ex. 49.   J. S. Bach, Fughetta, Allein Gott in der Höh' sei Ehr'

By resorting to this device, their entire expositions (and well beyond that point in Ex. 49) remain in the tonic key throughout. As we shall see, it is a subtlety whose point was missed completely by more than one theorist.

2.   SUBJECTS THAT OPEN WITH A DIRECT LEAP FROM TONIC TO DOMINANT

Regularly answered subjects (i.e. those that answer tonic and dominant tonally) need no explanation, and so discussion is centred on a relatively small group of so-called 'irregular' answers, for it is over these that many standard textbooks fall out both with each other, and at times even with the composer. The discussion is developed mainly around Prout's chapters on the Answer in his *Fugue;* firstly, because this textbook is still regarded in some quarters as a standard work on the subject, and secondly, because of the very obvious debt owed him by many subsequent writers.

The first structure to be discussed, is that which opens with a direct leap from tonic to dominant. We have already seen the textbook rule which is that subjects of this type should normally be replied to tonally, by a converse leap from dominant to tonic. First let

---

[2] This same reason almost certainly influenced Bach in the exposition of his D minor 'Fiddle' fugue, which is in the tonic key throughout. (See Ex. 110, p. 101).

[3] *Musical Textures*, pp. 24–25.

us consider the subject of Bach's 'short' G minor Organ Fugue, whose answer (a real one) has fascinated almost every writer on the subject.

Several explanations have been advanced since that of Richter, who, over a century ago wrote: 'if the subject begins with the notes of a complete chord it will be better that the commencement of the answer should represent a complete chord likewise; for example:—'

Ex. 50A. RICHTER, FROM CANON AND FUGUE

'In the same way the answer to Bach's fugue in G minor for the organ is as follows:—'[4]

Ex. 50B. J. S. BACH, ORGAN FUGUE IN G MINOR

(This example has been extended beyond Richter's quotation.)

As we shall see, Richter's theory came to be accepted as a principle by generations of subsequent writers on the subject.

Some few years later, Higgs gave a somewhat different explanation: 'Bach in answering his fugue subjects seems to have been very solicitous to retain the conjunct or disjunct form of his subject as far as possible. This consideration may explain his treatment of the answer in the Organ Fugue in G minor. . . . If Bach, instead of writing a real answer . . . had treated the subject tonally . . . the free springing figure of the subject would have been destroyed, and the imitation much disguised.'[5]

A. W. Marchant, whose *Five Hundred Fugue Subjects* is an elaboration of Higgs's chapter on the answer, attributes the real reply to the same cause—'probably in order to preserve the melodic character of subject in the answer.'[6]

Prout's explanation is quite different: 'Though the general practice of the great masters is . . . to answer the leap between tonic and dominant tonally, a real answer under such circumstances is not infrequent, especially when the leap is downwards.'[7]

Macpherson's explanation is different again: 'In many cases where the subject begins with the "arpeggio" of the Tonic chord, both Bach and other fugal writers adopt the more musical course of answering Tonic *harmony* by Dominant *harmony*.'[8]

[4] E. F. Richter, *Treatise on Canon and Fugue*, trans. F. Taylor, London, 1878, p. 52.
[5] J. Higgs, *Fugue*, London, 1878, p. 18.
[6] A. W. Marchant, *Five Hundred Fugue Subjects and Answers*, 2nd ed., London, 1892, p. 94.
[7] *Fugue*, p. 35, para. 91.
[8] *Counterpoint*, p. 102.

Kitson's reasoning is similar to Macpherson's: 'If, however, the leap to the dominant at the outset can be regarded as a good six-four, the Answer *can* be real. But Bach shows no consistency in the matter.

'For example, here are the Subject and Answer of an organ fugue. The Answer could have been tonal, but it is equally good as a real one.'[9] (Like Macpherson, Kitson here quotes the Subject and Answer of the 'short' G minor, showing the tonic chord of G minor as being answered by the dominant chord of D minor.)

Bairstow's explanation also follows that of Macpherson:

'When the dominant or dominant and tonic (*notes* not keys) occur as prominent sounds at the beginning of a subject, they are reversed in the answer—dominant answers tonic, tonic answers dominant.... These note changes are not arbitrary. In some cases they give variety and character to the answer; in others they spoil the contour. The latter is often the case when the notes of the tonic triad succeed each other.... Bach in his short organ fugue in G minor makes no note-alteration for this reason.'[10]

A. E. F. Dickinson advances an entirely different reason: 'The exceptions to this nearly all prove their case easily. [The] early G minor . . . has a five-bar subject, after which the caution of a tonal answer would be misplaced.'[11]

Oldroyd proposes a further new theory:

As one sees, Bach gives a real answer.... It was pointed out . . . that in all the eight cases in the '48' where a dominant note near the beginning of the subject was answered tonally, the reason was to main-tain Tonic tonality for a space after the Answer had entered. There was purpose in this, because the dominant key had not been reached, and a real answer would have disturbed or interfered with the smooth flow in the Tonic key and would have drawn attention to the move towards the dominant key. But the present case is quite different. There is no need for a Tonal Answer. Already the key of the dominant has been hinted at by the codetta . . . and no purpose would be served by melodic adjustment. The dominant key is being smoothly entered. Even if a Tonal answer had been chosen by Bach he could still have used a Dominant harmony $\sharp_4^6{}_2$ on G amounting to the same thing as a real answer.[12]

Hutchings's comments are perhaps best left until the next chapter. Not one of these theories can stand up to scrutiny. For example, both Higgs's and Prout's theories are demolished by the fact that many similarly constructed subjects are answered tonally:

EX. 51A.   J. S. BACH, CLAVIER SONATA IN D

EX. 51B.   J. S. BACH, THE ART OF FUGUE, CONTRAPUNCTUS I

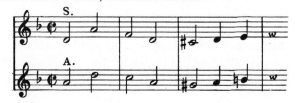

[9] *Fugal Construction*, p. 18.
[10] *Counterpoint and Harmony*, p. 320.
[11] *Bach's Fugal Works*, p. 165.
[12] *Technique and Spirit*, p. 89.

Ex. 51c.   Buxtehude, Chorale Prelude, Wie schön leuchtet der Morgenstern

Ex. 51d.   Righini, from A. W. Marchant's Fugue Subjects and Answers

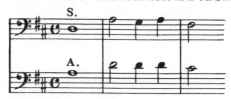

Ex. 51e.   Schwenke, from A. W. Marchant's Fugue Subjects and Answers

Ex. 51f.   Marpurg, From A. W. Marchant's Fugue Subjects and Answers

Ex. 51g.   A. W. Bach, from A. W. Marchant's Fugue Subjects and Answers

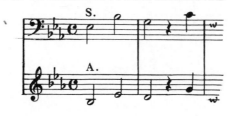

Ex. 51h.   Handel, Organ Concerto, No. 8 in A

Ex. 51I. J. S. Bach, Capriccio for Clavier in B flat

Ex. 51J. Schwenke, from A. W. Marchant's Fugue Subjects and Answers

This same group of tonally answered subjects serves also to demolish the tonic-triad theory of Richter, Macpherson, Kitson, and Bairstow. (Their theory is discussed fully later in this chapter.)

As for Dickinson's explanation, I personally fail to appreciate the influence of a subject's length over the form of its answer. Book II, No. 24 is a five-bar subject, yet it is answered tonally.

Oldroyd suggests that 'There is no need for a Tonal Answer. Already the key of the dominant has been hinted at by the codetta . . . and no purpose would be served by melodic adjustment. The dominant key is being smoothly entered.' In effect, Oldroyd is saying that once the dominant key has been reached, the need for a tonal answer does not arise. His argument is rendered unconvincing by the many examples of tonally answered subjects that can be quoted, modulation to the dominant key notwithstanding. Ex. 52a—52d gives some:

Ex. 52A. J. S. Bach, Musical Offering

Ex. 52B. J. S. Bach, Clavier Toccata in G

50

Ex. 52c. J. S. Bach, Clavier Fantasia and Fugue in A minor

Ex. 52d. J. S. Bach, Cantata, Ich hatte viel Bekümmernis

But the most doubtful of Oldroyd's statements is: 'Even if a Tonal answer had been chosen by Bach he could still have used a Dominant harmony $\sharp^{6}_{4}{}_{2}$ on G amounting to the same thing as a real answer.' For could he? Or perhaps we should ask, 'would he'? This question is asked, because one particular aspect of Baroque behaviour relating to fugal answer is likely to appear illogical, unless we appreciate the period's attitude regarding the dominant seventh chord. For similar reasons, contemporary usage of chords VII (major key) and II (minor key) must also be examined. The seemingly inconsistent answer to the subject now under discussion is a case in point. Contemporary usage of the dominant seventh and chord VII has, I feel, a direct bearing on this particular form of answer, and so at this point a diversion becomes necessary.

3. THE DOMINANT SEVENTH CHORD, AND DIMINISHED TRIAD IN BAROQUE THEORY AND PRACTICE

In Theory. I give extracts from one early, two mid-, and one late eighteenth-century theorists.

Godfrey Keller. Keller's rule relating to discords in general includes both the dominant seventh chord and the diminished triad: 'Discords are prepared by Concords, and resolved into Concords which are brought in when a part lies still.'[13] All sevenths in his examples are either prepared, or approached by step.

Marpurg. Sevenths. 'There are two cases in which the Seventh may appear unprepared. The first is *when one discord resolves on another*. This, however, takes place only in the free style. . . .'[14]

---

[13] G. Keller, *A Complete Method for Attaining to play a Thorough Bass*, London, 1707, p. 2, para. 2.
[14] Albrechtsberger defined the distinction between the 'free' and 'strict' styles thus: 'By the expression *strict composition*, is understood that which is produced for voices alone, without the accompaniment of any instrument. . . . When there is no instrumental accompaniment . . . dissonant skips or steps must be avoided . . . Nor must a discord be taken or quitted by a skip. . . . In strict composition every suspended discord should be prepared by a concord . . . Free composition is that in which . . . a discord may be employed without preparation . . .' (*Composition*, pp. 95–98.)

Ex. 53.   Marpurg, from Handbuch bey dem Generalbasse

    'The second case of unprepared discords occurs only in the case of certain Sevenths and their derivatives [i.e. inversions] in the free style. These Sevenths are: firstly that on the Dominant . . .

    'In the strict style on the other hand, all these Sevenths must be duly prepared, and, even in the free style, it is advisable in certain progressions that, even if the upper extreme of the Seventh is not prepared, at least the lower one should precede.'[15]

    Six-five chords. 'The Fifth in this chord represents the Seventh in the primary chord, and is dissonant. It must therefore be prepared and resolved. When imperfect [diminished], however (in which case the six-five is derived either from the dominant Seventh or the diminished Seventh), it can, in the free style, be taken unprepared. But just as, in the case of the chords of the Seventh which can be struck unprepared, it is advisable that the Bass should be retained from the previous chord: so, too, in the case of six-five chords, it is advisable that the Sixth should be there beforehand.'[16]

    Four-three, and six-four-two chords. Marpurg's recommendations are in all respects similar to those relating to seventh, and six-five chords.[17]

    C. P. E. Bach. C. P. E. Bach's explanation is thorough, detailed, and liberally illustrated with musical examples. Coming from a composer of his stature, it may be accepted as authoritative.

    Chords of the seventh. 'The seventh is a dissonance which appears with preparation . . . and without it.'

Ex. 54a.   C. P. E. Bach, from The True Art of Playing Keyboard Instruments

Ex. 54b.   ibid.

'It progresses by stepwise descent.'[18]

    The Six-five chord. 'The fifth is treated as a dissonance. It is usually restricted by the sixth,[19] and always progresses by stepwise descent. . . . the diminished fifth may lie in the preceding chord or enter freely. However, when this latter interval is taken unprepared, the sixth is usually present in the preceding chord.'[20]

---

[15] C. F. Arnold, *The Art of Accompaniment from a Thorough-Bass*, London, 1931, p. 545.
[16] p. 602.
[17] pp. 628 and 648.
[18] C. P. E. Bach, *Essay on the True Art of Playing Keyboard Instruments*, trans. and ed. W. J. Mitchell, 2nd. ed., London, 1951, p. 265.
[19] C. P. E. Bach adds a footnote 'i.e., except when the sixth is omitted, when the fifth is diminished (in which case it is already a dissonance, hence, restricted anyway), or when the chord is a "passing chord".' p. 244).
[20] p. 244.

The Four-three chord. 'The exceptional features of the chord are that the third [i.e. the seventh from the root] is treated as a dissonance and the fourth enjoys more freedom than usual. . . . When the chord consists of a major sixth, perfect fourth, and minor third, either the fourth or the third must be prepared. Most frequently it is the third, which then moves by stepwise descent.'[21]

The chord of the second. ($^4_2$ and $^6_4$). 'The dissonance is in the bass and may enter as either a tied note . . . or a passing tone, but it always resolves by stepwise descent.'[22]

Ex. 55A. IBID.

Ex. 55B. IBID.[23]

(It will be noticed that the seventh is more restricted in this inversion than in the root position, or in the other inversions; also, that C. P. E. Bach is stricter here than Marpurg. It will be seen that Bach's theories are closely in step with contemporary practice.)

Although not published until 1791, Türk's recommendations regarding the chord of the dominant seventh both in root position and in inversions admit to no relaxations over those of earlier theorists; that where possible the seventh should be prepared 'particularly in strict style . . . yet sometimes it also occurs freely',[24] in which event Türk recommends the preparation of the fundamental of the chords, which is little different from Marpurg's caution 'the lower one should precede'. Indeed, although not appearing until some three decades later, Türk's recommendations in general regarding the dominant seventh chord in both root position and inversions are no different from those of Marpurg.[25]

Particularly illuminating are Thomas Attwood's observations concerning the dominant seventh chord, as he recorded these while studying under Mozart. 'In Case of Necessity *neither* the 7th nor any of those Chords derived from it are obliged to be prepared. Yet, tis allways better when they are.'[26]

And this as late as 1785!

The diminished triad. (*a*) *Root position.*

C. P. E. Bach. 'The diminished fifth is a dissonance which is introduced with preparation [Ex.56a] or without it [Ex. 56b].'[27]

Ex. 56A. IBID.

---

[21] pp. 233–4.
[22] p. 253.
[23] p. 255, fig. 327.
[24] D. G. Türk, *Kurze Anweisung zum Generalbassspielen*, Leipzig, 1791, Chap. V, *Abschnitt* (Section) I, p. 159, para. 119.
[25] See pp. 174, 183, and 191 of same chapter.
[26] *Kompositionsstudien*, p. 36.
[27] *Art of Playing Keyboard Instruments*, p. 223.

Ex. 56B. IBID.

' A leap may be made to an unprepared diminished fifth.'

Ex. 56C. IBID.

Ex. 56D. IBID.

'As part of a triad this dissonance is treated more freely than in other relationships.'[28]
(*b*) *Second inversion*

The only references to the diminished triad in its second inversion encountered by the writer were concerned with II, minor key. These came from C.P.E.Bach[29] and Türk. The latter writes: 'The six-four chord, derived from the diminished triad by second inversion, with major sixth and augmented fourth seldom occurs.'[30]

The musical examples given by both writers restrict the use of this inversion to its being preceded and followed by root position or first inversion of the same chord—i.e. in arpeggio fashion.

In Practice. The part played by Monteverdi in freeing the seventh of V[7] from preparation finds frequent mention in histories of music. Ethel Home[31] quotes an example of a seventh being struck simultaneously with the dominant triad:

Ex. 57A. MONTEVERDI, FROM ETHEL HOME'S SHORT HISTORY OF MUSIC

Dyson's quotation shows a far more adventurous experiment:

Ex. 57B. MONTEVERDI, MADRIGAL, CRUDA AMARILLI

[28] p. 224.
[29] pp. 229–30, para. 13, Fig. 286(c).
[30] *Generalbassspielen*, pp. 147–8, para. 111, Exx. b and c.
[31] E. Home, *Short History of Music*, London, 1926, p. 58.

Dyson comments, 'Thus Monteverdi, with daring, but with prophetic truth, wrote the following, in which a seventh of this kind is struck independently.'[32]

Frequent reference to Monteverdi's innovation has had the effect of misleading some (the writer included) into believing that henceforth the unprepared seventh of the dominant discord was to become part of everyday musical language. The truth is very different.

The Dominant Seventh in seventeenth- and eighteenth-century practice. The following works were examined:

Buxtehude (1637–1707). Vols I and II of the Organ Works. (Novello.)

Corelli (1653–1713). *Sonate da chiesa* of 1683 (Op. I) and 1689 (Op. III); *Sonate da camera* of 1685 (Op. II) and 1694 (Op. IV); Sonatas for Violin and Cembalo (Op. V); Twelve Concerti Grossi of 1712 (Op. VI).

Vivaldi (1675–1741). Nos. 2, 6, 8, 10, 11, and 12 of Op. 3. (Solo and Grosso Concerti.)

Handel. Twelve Concerti Grossi (Op. 6), and *Messiah*.

Bach. St John and *St Matthew* Passions.

These works thus span the greater part of a century.

Buxtehude. Root position and first inversion.[33] Almost invariably, the seventh is either prepared, or approached by step. Instances of the seventh taken by leap are rare.

Third inversion. Not one example was found of the seventh taken by leap.[34] Invariably, the seventh is either prepared or approached by step. It is interesting to recall that Buxtehude died in 1707, exactly 100 years after the appearance of Monteverdi's *Orfeo*!

Corelli. Root position and first inversion. His approach is, if anything, more strict than that of Buxtehude, for only some half-dozen instances were encountered of the seventh being introduced other than by preparation, or by step. Even when taken by leap, they were generally the outcome of sequence.

Ex. 58A.   CORELLI, CONCERTO GROSSO, OP. 6, NO. 7

Apart from these, only two instances were found of the seventh taken by leap:

Ex. 58B.   CORELLI, SONATA DA CAMERA, Op. 2, No. 6

---

[32] *Grove*, 3rd ed., London, 1929, II, p. 530.

[33] Although Marpurg and C. P. E. Bach both give recommendations regarding the $V^6_{4\;3}$ chord, its use in the Baroque is comparatively rare. Discussion is therefore limited to the chord's root position, and first and third inversions.

[34] This is not to claim that such examples do not exist. They possibly do, but after my own search, I hardly feel it a pastime I can wholeheartedly recommend.

Ex. 58C. CORELLI, CONCERTO GROSSO, Op. 6, No. 4

Third inversion. As with Buxtehude, no examples were found of the seventh taken by leap.

Vivaldi. Root position and first inversion. Again, very rarely does one come across the seventh being taken by leap.

Third inversion. As with Buxtehude and Corelli, not a single example was found of the seventh being approached by leap.

Handel. Root position and first inversion. In both *Messiah* and the twelve Concerti Grossi, there is a slightly freer approach, more so in the instrumental than in the vocal medium. Even so, in the vast majority of cases the seventh is either prepared or approached by step. Throughout the whole of *Messiah* for example, barely a dozen cases were found of the seventh being approached by leap.

Third inversion. In *Messiah*, only two cases of the seventh being approached by leap were found, and it is significant that both occur in continuo accompaniment to recitatives:

Ex. 59A. HANDEL, MESSIAH

Ex. 59B. IBID.

Although more freedom of approach is seen in the instrumental Concerti Grossi, the group yielded fewer than half-a-dozen examples of the seventh being taken by leap, of which some were no more than the result of transference of discord.

Bach. Root position and first inversion. Bach's behaviour is somewhat more relaxed than Handel's, but here again, in the great majority of instances, the seventh is either prepared, or approached by step.

Third inversion. Bach is again slightly less strict than his contemporary; but only slightly less, for in the vast majority of cases his approach to the bass note of the third inversion is no different from that of other of his contemporaries. His approach may be briefly summarized thus: in the great majority of cases the bass note is either prepared or approached by step. In the comparatively few cases where he approaches it by leap,[35] he sounds the seventh or root of V⁷ in the previous chord:

Ex. 60A.   J. S. Bach, St Matthew Passion

Ex. 60B.   J. S. Bach, St John Passion

So that, well over 100 years after Monteverdi's challenge, the seventh is still viewed with the utmost respect. The Baroque in general apparently felt but little urge to exploit his innovation.

The diminished chord (VII, and II minor key) in root position and second inversion.[36]

Handel. Root position. In *Messiah* some score or so examples of the diminished triad were found, and in the majority of cases, the diminished fifth is either prepared or approached by step. Unprepared fifths are usually the result of sequence, and the only true example found of the unprepared discord is given in Ex. 61, which the ear readily accepts as the seventh of V⁷:

Ex. 61.   Handel, Messiah

Second inversion. No examples of this were encountered.

Bach. (*St John Passion*, and a group of chorales.) *Root position.* Very few examples of its use in root position were found, and in most of these the diminished fifth is either prepared or approached by step. As with Handel, the unprepared discord is generally the result of sequence. Ex. 62 gives one of the very rare instances found of the diminished fifth taken by leap, when it is merely part of an appoggiatura chord:

---

[35] Thus Marpurg (see pp. 51-52).
[36] Contemporary use of the first inversion of the diminished chord is too familiar to warrant discussion.

Ex. 62. J. S. Bach, Chorale, Ich ruf zu dir, Herr Jesu Christ

Second inversion. The only example found is from a recitative in *St John Passion*. It is really no more than the second inversion of the common chord of E flat, coloured by a chromatic passing note:

Ex. 63. J. S. Bach, St John Passion

To summarize, the normal procedure in root position is either to prepare the discord, or approach it by step. Only very rarely does one come across the diminished fifth being approached by leap. The approach by leap to the bass note of a diminished chord in its second inversion may fairly be discounted, as it was clearly beyond the period's technique.[37]

Now, throughout the course of the 'short' G minor Organ Fugue, the second note of subject and answer alike is harmonized by chord V. A tonal reply at either of the answer's appearances in the exposition (Ex. 64a and 64b) would result in an approach by leap to the bass note of VII$^6_4$, or, if you will, to the bass note of implied V$\sharp^6_2$—progressions beyond the normal technique of the period:

Ex. 64A. J. S. Bach, Organ Fugue in G minor

Ex. 64B. ibid.

[37] The sole example encountered by the writer is in Var. X (bar three) of Bach's *Aria and Ten Variations in the Italian Style* for clavier (BWV 989), but even this case should be viewed in relation to its immediate context.

(See also Exx. 29, bar 51, p. 29, and 100b viola entry, p. 91, whose harmonic conditions at the respective answers' point of entry are identical. It is not an accident surely, that all three composers shy at giving a tonal answer.)

The writer himself is thoroughly convinced that it is these harmonic implications, and not any of the various theories quoted at the commencement of this discussion, that may be held to account for Bach's real answer.

When attempting to disprove theories that have held sway over the greater part of a century, one cannot be expected to establish an entirely new one on the strength of a solitary example. Supporting evidence is therefore given, and is developed from two different angles.

A first and obvious step, is to produce further subjects and answers that resemble the 'short' G minor Organ Fugue. This presents no difficulty, and they will be examined later.

A second, and not so obvious step, suggests itself through Oldroyd's observation that '. . . he [Bach] could still have used a . . . $V^6_{\sharp 4 2}$ on G'. In saying this, Oldroyd accepts the formula in Ex. 65 (the approach to the bass note of V^4_2 by leap) as normal Baroque practice.

Ex. 65.

Eight fugues were found whose openings have the same melodic shape as that of the 'short' G minor. They are, Contrapunctus I and II of *The Art of Fugue*, Book I, No. 17, Ex. 66a and 66b, and Ex. 51a, 51h and 51i (pp. 48-50):

Ex. 66A.   BUXTEHUDE, ORGAN FUGUE IN C

Ex. 66B.   J. S. BACH, EIGHT LITTLE PRELUDES AND FUGUES, No. 5 IN G

All eight subjects are answered *tonally*, so that, according to Oldroyd's reasoning, the second note of their respective answers when appearing in the lowest part could be regarded as the bass note of a potential V^4_2 chord. Yet in all eight answers their respective composers consistently *avoid* this. Take, for example, the subject and answer that serve for both Contrapunctus I and II of *The Art of Fugue*:

59

Ex. 67. J. S. BACH, THE ART OF FUGUE, CONTRAPUNCTUS I

As will be seen, it is answered tonally, thus creating a potential opening for a V_2^4 chord on its second note. Altogether there are ten harmonized entries of the subject using the same melodic shape as the subject of the 'short' G minor Organ Fugue, and without exception its second note is harmonized by chord V.[38] There are three entries of the answer whose second note creates a potential V_2^4 chord at the corresponding point, as in Ex. 65 on p. 59.[39] The fact that Bach consistently avoids using the V_2^4 chord at these points cannot be dismissed as mere coincidence.

Next, consideration was given to another formula which creates a similar potential opening for a V_2^4 chord:

Ex. 68. BUXTEHUDE, ORGAN PRELUDE AND FUGUE IN G MINOR

A group of fugues with openings similar to the example from Buxtehude was examined:

Buxtehude. Organ Works, Vol. II (Preludes and Fugues) (Novello), fugues Nos. 7, 12a, 14 and 22.

Bach. *Eight Little Preludes and Fugues*, No. 2 in D minor (BWV 554); *Organ Fugue in E major* (BWV 566); *Organ Fugue in G minor* (BWV 542); *Organ Fugue in A minor* (BWV 551); *Organ Fugue in G major* (BWV 550); Book I, No. 24.

Handel. Concerti Grossi (Op. 6), Nos. 2, 3, and 7; *Fugue* from Clavier Suite No. 6 in F sharp minor; *Fugue* in G, and *Fughetta* in C for Clavier.

Although presenting numerous opportunities, not one case was found of an answer's opening note harmonized as V_2^4, unless, as in the example from Buxtehude, the seventh was first prepared. As in the case of the formula in Ex. 65, the result of the present examination assumes added significance when it is pointed out that the corresponding note (i.e. the initial note) of the several *subjects* in this group, far more often than not, *is* harmonized by V. BWV 566 in particular will well repay study in this respect. This fresh evidence it is hoped, gives further proof of the period's reluctance to approach the bass note of a V_2^4 chord by leap, or to commence with a V_2^4 chord without due preparation of the seventh. More important still, it lends considerable support to the writer's theory relating to the answer of the 'short' G minor Organ Fugue.

We now come to examine a group of 'irregularly' answered subjects that has much in common with the subject of the 'short' G minor. One similarity is the melodic curve of their first few notes. This same feature characterizes the group in Ex. 51 on pp. 48–50, but the fundamental difference between the two groups is that, whereas in Ex. 51 harmonic

---

[38] Contrapunctus I, bars 9, 23, 29, 56; and II, bars 9, 23, 31, 45, 61, 79. (Boosey and Hawkes edition.)
[39] I, bars 13, 32; II, bar 38.

considerations do not stand in the way of tonal answers, in the group that follows they do; so that in this respect too, there is affinity with the 'short' G minor.

The first example is Bach's G major Organ Fugue (Ex. 69a) which, surprisingly, appears to have escaped every theorist's attention; surprisingly, because it has so much in common with the oft-quoted G minor. First, the melodic contour of its opening three notes. Secondly, that throughout its course, the second note of both subject and answer almost as consistently is harmonized by dominant harmony; and thirdly, that its opening leap of a fifth from tonic to dominant is not replied to tonally. A tonal answer at its first appearance in bar seven would have involved a leap to the fifth of the diminished triad, which was precisely the case in the G minor:

Ex. 69A.   J. S. Bach, Organ Fugue in G

At the answer's second appearance in bar 25 (Ex. 69b) a tonal reply would have meant approaching the bass note of a V^4_2 chord by leap:

Ex. 69B.   ibid.

and at its third appearance in bar 63, the fifth of V^6_5 by leap:

Ex. 69C.   ibid.

Bach avoids these situations by the expedient of real answer. It therefore follows that in this instance Bach regards the harmonization of his subject as relatively more important than replying to it tonally. It is a further instance of what was said earlier, that a tonal answer was not permitted to stand in the way of spontaneous musical impulse.

Another close parallel is contained in a fugue by Pachelbel. Throughout its course, the fifth note in subject and answer alike bears some form of dominant harmony:

Ex. 70.   PACHELBEL, ORGAN FUGUE IN E MINOR

A tonal reply at the answer's first appearance in bar four would have involved a leap to the fifth of the diminished triad; (i.e. implied VII$_4^6$); although it may be argued that the suspensions in bars eleven and eighteen render tonal answers possible, nevertheless, real answers are given in both instances. Precisely the same reasons preclude a tonal reply to the subject of Bach's A minor Clavier Fugue. The resemblance in the melodic curve of its first few notes to Pachelbel's subject will not pass unnoticed:

Ex. 71A.   J. S. BACH, CLAVIER FUGUE IN A MINOR

Tonal answers are obviously avoided in later appearances of the answer for similar reasons:

Ex. 71B.   IBID.

bar 44

Ex. 71C.   IBID.

bar 54

Similarly, the harmony stands in the way of a tonal answer to the subject of the C minor Organ Fugue:

Ex. 72.   J. S. BACH, ORGAN PASSACAGLIA AND FUGUE IN C MINOR

63

The same reasons might be advanced to account for the real answer in Ex. 73, which is quoted by Prout:[40]

EX. 73.   HANDEL, CONCERTO GROSSO, OP. 6, NO. 1 IN G

In common with the group just examined, the dominant note is harmonized by V, which in the case of a tonal response being given, again would involve approaching the seventh of V[7] by leap; it would also result in some poor part-writing. These considerations apart, some theorists hold the same view as Prout, that a real answer is given here 'because the subject begins with the notes of the tonic chord'. This theory is about to be discussed, but in passing, two subjects and answers by Murschhauser (1663–1738) and Beethoven respectively are given. (Exx. 74 and 75.) It will be seen that although the contour of their respective openings are similar to Ex. 73 from Handel, nevertheless they run counter to Prout's theory:

EX. 74. MURSCHHAUSER, FROM OCTI-TONIUM NOVUM ORGÁNICUM

---

[40] *Fugue*, pp. 37–38, paras. 94–95.

Ex. 75. BEETHOVEN, DIABELLI VARIATIONS

A third supporting example is Book II, No. 21.

Finally, refer back to Ex. 27 on pp. 26–27. Although not strictly of the type of structure under discussion (i.e. a direct leap from tonic to dominant), the same principles of tonal answer normally would apply. The extract is to the final exposition entry. As in this extract, the third note of the ensuing seven entries of subject and answer alike is harmonized by chord V. It thus follows that a tonal answer, which normally one would expect, would involve a leap to the seventh of V⁷. Yet again, a real reply is given at each of the answer's five appearances.

To summarize, a group of subjects has just been quoted possessing certain features common to each other, and to the 'short' G minor Organ Fugue. As in the G minor, their respective openings are marked by a leap from tonic to dominant; their respective dominant notes are associated with some form of dominant harmony, and as in the G minor they are all given real answers. Collectively, the evidence is too consistent to be dismissed as mere coincidence.

Further evidence of a similar nature is advanced in the section that follows.

4. SUBJECTS THAT OPEN WITH NOTES OF THE TONIC CHORD, COMMENCING ON THE TONIC.

In the earlier discussion of Bach's real answer to the subject of the 'short' G minor Organ Fugue, attention was drawn to Richter's recommendation relating to a subject that begins with 'the notes of a complete chord': 'it will be better that the commencement of the answer should represent a complete chord likewise.' (See Ex. 50a on p. 47, and compare with Exx. 76, and 82e on p. 71.)

With so much evidence to the contrary, it is remarkable that Richter's recommendation should have become so widely accepted, and allowed to pass without serious challenge for over a century. It would be no easy matter to find a more curious misunderstanding of musical practice by theory, than that which has arisen around subjects and answers of this type. No less curious is the number of subsequent writers who have subscribed to Richter's theory. Thus Prout:

When the tonic goes to the dominant through the third of the scale, the rule of the old text-books is that the answer should be tonal. We give two examples by Bach—

Ex. 76. J. S. BACH, FOUR DUETS, No. 2 IN F

[See also Ex. 52d on p. 51]

In both these cases the dominant is answered by the tonic. But these subjects belong to a large class —those that begin with the notes of the tonic chord taken in succession. In such cases the great masters give a real answer nearly, if not quite, as often as a tonal one. . . .

We now give a number of examples where the leap between tonic and dominant has a real answer, because the subject begins with the notes of the tonic chord—

Ex. 77A. J. S. Bach, Cantata, Es ist dir gesagt

Ex. 77B. J. S. Bach, Cantata, Bringet dem Herrn Ehre seines Namens

Ex. 77C. J. S. Bach, Clavier Sonata in D

Ex. 77D. Handel, Israel in Egypt

Ex. 77E. Handel, Organ Concerto No. 9 in B flat

Ex. 77F. Handel, Concerto Grosso, Op. 6, No. 1 in G

In the works of Handel we find a real answer in such cases even more frequently than in the works of Bach. . . .

If we examine and compare all the examples we have given of subjects founded upon the notes of the tonic chord, and taking real answers, we shall find that there is an important principle involved in all of them. We have already shown that the tonal answer is the result of the old modal systems which prevailed before modern tonality, as now understood, was fixed. In all these cases, however, the old rule gives way to a higher and more important law . . . This is the broad principle which is the very basis of fugal answer—that tonic harmony should be answered by dominant, and dominant by tonic.[41]

Prout sums up with this odd rule: '*If a subject commence with the leap from tonic to dominant, and the following note is not a note of the tonic chord, a tonal answer is generally, though not invariably, preferable; but if at least the first three notes of the subject are all notes of the tonic chord, the answer, provided that no modulation takes place to the key of the dominant, may be either real or tonal.*'[42]

His rule is characteristic of the equivocal nature of the theory that it supplements, and although given 'for the guidance of the student', it is hardly helpful. For example, he gives no specific reason for his caution 'provided that no modulation takes place to the key of the dominant'. His proviso is difficult to understand, especially when we come across real and tonal answers to modulating and non-modulating subjects alike. The openings of Ex. 78a and 78b are both founded on 'notes of the tonic chord', yet the former is given a tonal, and the latter a real answer. Both these are non-modulating subjects:

Ex. 78A.   J. S. Bach, 'Forty-Eight', Book I, No. 17

Ex. 78B.   Purcell, Ten Sonatas of Four Parts, No. 7

Conversely, Ex. 79a and 79b both modulate to the key of the dominant; yet the former is given a tonal answer, and the latter a real one. This is, however, only a side issue:

Ex. 79A.   J. S. Bach, Organ Toccata and Fugue in C

[41] pp. 36–40, paras. 92–100.
[42] p. 40, para. 101. (Prout's italics.)

F

In a previous chapter (p. 15), we saw Macpherson 'correcting' Bach's answer to the subject of his *Musical Offering*, from a tonal to a real one 'mainly for the reason that the very clear movement of the first three notes through the Tonic chord of C minor almost compels us to wish for a corresponding movement in the answer through the Tonic chord of G minor.' [43] A later observation shows his indebtedness to Prout when he says, 'In many cases where the subject begins with the 'arpeggio' of the Tonic chord, both Bach and other fugal writers adopt the more musical course of answering Tonic *harmony* by Dominant *harmony*.'[44] We saw on p. 48 that Bairstow also imputes the real answer in the 'short' G minor Organ Fugue to this same cause. A more recent writer who keeps this theory alive is A. J. B. Hutchings, when he says:

> To use a tonal answer when a real one would be less awkward is to be like a jackass who would rather squash a whole bevy of ladies while opening a door than get out of the room first. A tonal answer may prevent an uncomfortable six-four, awkward or fussy modulation, or melodic poverty; but with some subjects it will produce these very faults. The convention should be jettisoned, for instance, if the opening of S announces *all* the notes of a tonic triad in ascending or descending order, or uses the mediant prominently along with the tonic and dominant. . . .
>
> The subjects quoted [see Ex. 80a and 80b] have a melodic shape and harmonic vigour to which only an insensitive musician would respond with a tonal answer; but perhaps such an answer would be made by a sensitive student afraid, like our door-opening friend, of breaking a convention.[45]

Ex. 80A. PURCELL, TEN SONATAS OF FOUR PARTS, NO. 5

Ex. 80B. PURCELL, TEN SONATAS OF FOUR PARTS, NO. 7

In common with Bairstow, he attributes the real answer of the 'short' G minor Organ Fugue to this cause (its 'tonic triad' opening), and follows Oldroyd's line of reasoning by concluding, 'Dominant tonality is established from the first note of Bach's answer. Though he could have made his second note G, his deference to convention would have been like that of the gallant door-opener.'[46] Hutchings rounds off this part of his chapter on the answer with, 'but you are still a crude sort of musician if you prefer a tonal answer to a real answer in [Ex. 80b]'.[47]

---

[43] *Counterpoint*, p. 102. The electrifying effect of the tonal answer in performance, is in itself sufficient justification surely for its existence!
[44] p. 102.
[45] *Invention and Composition*, pp. 84–85.
[46] p. 87.
[47] p. 87.

I therefore stand self-condemned when I confess that had I to choose between giving a real or tonal answer to Purcell's subject, provided that the choice was to be influenced solely by *melodic* considerations, then I would unhesitatingly align myself with Hutchings's 'gallant door-opening friend'—a decision I hope to justify.

As a result of my own research into the matter, I am fully convinced that 'the rule of the old text-books', as Prout terms it, was just as alive and respected in Bach's day, as when it was originally formulated; and that Prout was quite wrong in supplanting it by his own theory, which is tantamount to a complete reversal of the original rule—'procedure' is perhaps a more appropriate term.

I found ample proof that subjects commencing with this melodic formula were viewed no differently from those opening with a direct leap from tonic to dominant, of which it is merely a variant; and what has been said in connection with the latter type applies equally to the former, that when appropriate, and provided harmonic and melodic considerations did not intervene, it was the tonal, and not the real answer that constituted normal procedure; even so, the claim of tonal answer was never given priority over spontaneous musical impulse. It will be shown that the real answers quoted by Prout, Hutchings and others, do not constitute 'normal procedure' but are the outcome of melody's deference to harmony. What was said about carrying tonic tonality into the answer, also applies here. Good examples of this are Book I, No. 17, Contrapunctus IV of *The Art of Fugue*, and Ex. 81, in which tonic tonality is maintained throughout the exposition.

Ex. 81.   BUXTEHUDE, ORGAN TOCCATA IN F

Prout asserts, 'In the works of Handel we find a real answer in such cases even more frequently than in the works of Bach.'[48] This view is upheld by Dent when he writes, 'Prout points out that Handel shows a great partiality for real answers, and Handel's authority is surely as good as anyone else's.'[49] Whether or not this be correct is unimportant, and may be dismissed as coincidental, as my own experience suggests that the behaviour of neither of these composers is any more, or any less, regular than that of the other. Again, Prout's observation, 'In such cases the great masters give a real answer nearly, if not quite, as often as a tonal one', is not only questionable but meaningless, in that even if this were so, it still proves nothing.

The great weakness of the 'tonic-triad' theory is that none of the writers who subscribe to it has seriously attempted to account for the very great number of instances in which the 'tonic-triad' formula is replied to *tonally*. They have either preserved silence on the matter, or criticized examples that run counter to their own theory, which in turn becomes weakened through the limiting of its explanation to real answers only. Refer back, for example, to the group in Ex. 51a–51j on pp. 48–50, and Ex. 31a–31c on p. 33; they all, to re-quote Hutchings, 'announce all the notes of a tonic triad in ascending or descending order', yet all are answered tonally; and there scarcely could be a piece of more convincing evidence to the contrary of the tonic-triad theory than Ex. 52d on p. 51.

Several more tonally-answered subjects of this type are given in Ex. 82a–82o, and many more could be added.

Ex. 82A. J. S. Bach, Concerto for Two Claviers in C

Ex. 82B. J. S. Bach, Capriccio for Clavier in E

Ex. 82C. J. S. Bach, Musical Offering

[48] *Fugue*, pp. 37–38, para. 95.
[49] *Notes on Fugue*, p. 21.

Ex. 82d.   J. S. Bach, 'Forty-Eight', Book II, No. 3

Ex. 82e.   Schwenke, Fugue in B flat

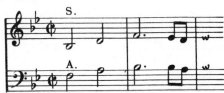

Ex. 82f.   Schwenke, Fugue in C

Ex. 82g.   J. G. Walther, Preludio con Fuga

Ex. 82h.   Haydn, Mass in C

Ex. 82i.   Pachelbel, Chorale Prelude, Wie schön leuchtet der Morgenstern

Ex. 82J.   MENDELSSOHN, FROM A. W. MARCHANT'S FUGUE SUBJECTS AND ANSWERS

Ex. 82K.   GOTTLIEB MUFFAT, FROM A. W. MARCHANT'S FUGUE SUBJECTS AND ANSWERS

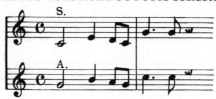

Ex. 82L.   SALA, FROM A. W. MARCHANT'S FUGUE SUBJECTS AND ANSWERS

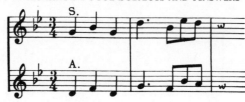

Ex. 82M.   J. S. BACH, CHORALE PRELUDE, WIE SCHÖN LEUCHT'T UNS DER MORGENSTERN

Ex. 82N.   J. S. BACH, CHORALE PRELUDE, IN DICH HAB' ICH GEHOFFET, HERR

Ex. 82O.   W. F. BACH, FROM A. W. MARCHANT'S FUGUE SUBJECTS AND ANSWERS

Collectively this group poses some awkward questions. Of Hutchings, for example, why in all these cases was the convention of tonal reply not jettisoned? And the same of Macpherson, who recommends a real reply in such cases as 'the more musical course'. Likewise of Prout, concerning his claim 'the old rule gives way to a higher and more important law . . . that tonic harmony should be answered by dominant, and dominant by tonic.'

Examination will show that the reasons accounting for real answers to subjects of this type are no different from those behind real answers to the type that opens with a direct leap from tonic to dominant. More frequently than not, the real answer is the direct consequence of harmonic implications. It was this surely, and not unwillingness on his part to weaken either its 'melodic shape' or its 'harmonic vigour' that induced Purcell to give a real answer to the subject in Ex. 80b on p. 68. As Bach in the 'short' G minor Organ Fugue harmonizes its second note (the dominant) with dominant harmony, so Purcell in the *Canzona* (Ex. 80b) harmonizes its fifth note (in subject and answer alike) by V, thus precluding the possibility of tonal reply. Attempts to answer his subject tonally would result in such situations as in Ex. 83a, 83b, and 83c.:

Ex 83A.

Ex. 83B.

Ex. 83C.

If, as Hutchings claims, 'you are still a crude sort of musician if you prefer a tonal answer to a real answer in [Ex. 80b]', then how would he account for the *tonal* answers to the subjects in Ex. 82a, 82b, 82d, 82l, and 82n (pp. 70–72), whose features bear a strong likeness (82a, 82l, and 82n particularly so) to Purcell's subject, and yet whose answers without exception are *tonal*? The fundamental difference between Purcell's harmonic texture and that say, of the C major *Concerto for Two Claviers and Orchestra*, is that whereas the former precludes a tonal answer, the latter allows one. Had not Purcell's harmonies stood in the way of a tonal answer, then it might not be unreasonable to suggest that his reply might have taken on a tonal form as in Ex. 84, which is exactly as given by Bach to the Two-clavier Concerto subject (see Ex. 82a).

Ex. 84.

In its new guise, it loses nothing by way of 'melodic shape' or 'harmonic vigour' the writer suggests, than is lost by Bach's answer in the Concerto. Incidentally, the Purcell example (Ex. 80b) lends further strong support to the writer's theory concerning Bach's answer in the 'short' G minor Organ Fugue, in that certain of their features—the prominence of their respective dominant notes, their consistent dominant harmonizations, and their real replies, are identical.

The real answer in Ex. 85a is in similar case to Exx. 18 on p. 23, and 20b on p. 24, in that it is compelled to take its form from the cadential harmonies. In turn, those in Ex. 85b, 85c, 85d, and 85e are in similar case to Exx. 25, 26, 27, 28 on pp. 26–27, and 80a and 80b on p. 68; in all these examples, a tonal reply must result in the answer entering on, or leaping to the diminished fifth of the bare tritone (implied VIIa), or in an implied VII$^6_4$ chord, or in both. For example, attempted tonal replies in bars three and nine of Ex. 85d would produce respectively, an implied and an expressed VII$^6_4$ chord:

Ex. 85A.   Handel, Israel in Egypt

Ex. 85B.   J. S. Bach, Chorale Prelude, Herr Jesu Christ, dich zu uns wend'

Ex. 85C.   J. Christoph Bach, Herr Jesu Christ, dich zu uns wend'

Ex. 85D.   Pachelbel, Interludes to the Magnificat, I. 6

Ex. 85E. HANDEL, CLAVIER FUGUE IN D

These, clearly, are the apparent reasons; from the uniform pattern of behaviour, it is equally clear that their respective composers are unanimous in their reluctance to use the bare tritone—hence the consistency of real reply.

In support of this assertion a piece of purely fortuitous but highly interesting evidence is thrown up by two different versions of the eighteenth bar of Handel's Concerto Grosso IV, of Op. 3. The version quoted by Prout[50] (Ex. 86a) follows Chrysander's edition, which Dr Frederick Hudson suggests is founded solely on a Walsh print, probably of c.1752; the version given in the recently-published *Hallische Händel-Ausgabe* (Ex. 86b) follows (i) the authoritative copy of Concertos I, II and IV (Fitzwilliam Museum); (ii) complete copy of all Concertos in Op. 3 (British Museum) and (iii) copy of Concerto IV as in the *Ode for Queen Anne's Birth Day* (B.M.).[51]

Ex. 86A. HANDEL, CONCERTO GROSSO, OP. 3, No. 4 IN F

Ex. 86B. IBID.

The weighty evidence of Dr Hudson's research should put beyond doubt that the H. H.-A. version is the authorative one.

The alteration of the B flat into B natural by the Walsh print editor was done, obviously, to guide the tonality into C major for the entry of the answer. But why should this same editor have considered it necessary apparently to make the *double* alteration by changing first violin's F to a G? My contention is that the F was altered to a G because the answer must otherwise enter on the unprepared diminished fifth of the bare tritone, which as already pointed out is rarely to be seen in the period's music. Put the other way, had this progression (involving the diminished fifth) been in keeping with normal contemporary technique, the second alteration, surely, would not have been considered necessary.

It is a little ironic that Prout destroys his own 'tonic-triad' theory by one of the very examples with which he attempts to establish it. I refer to his quotation of Handel's Concerto Grosso No. 1 in G of Op. 6 (Ex. 73, p. 64), for later in the same movement we find a free inversion of the original subject, being answered *tonally*:

[50] *Fugue*, p. 43, para. 105b.
[51] *Hallische Händel-Ausgabe*, IV/II, *Kritischer Bericht*, Kassel, 1963, pp. 50–52, and p. 93.

Ex. 87. HANDEL, CONCERTO GROSSO, OP. 6, NO. 1 IN G

Prout himself may have been quite unaware of this, but it is questionable whether Handel would discard the 'old rule' in favour of a 'higher and more important law', only to commit a turn about face within the same movement. The very fact of his answering the inverted form of this subject *tonally* rules out surely, Prout's 'notes of the tonic chord' theory. This contention draws strong support from Variation XXIV of the *Diabelli Variations* (Ex. 75, p. 65), for although the melodic shape of its opening is identical with that of Ex. 73, Beethoven answers it tonally, 'notes of the tonic chord' notwithstanding. It is merely a question of the harmonic situations that these subjects' respective counterpoints create, for whereas one (Ex. 87) admits a tonal reply, the other (Ex. 73), as already explained on p. 64, does not. In similar case is Book II, No. 21.

Ex. 88 experiments by adapting Beethoven's contrapuntal *idea* to a *tonal* answer to the subject of Ex. 73:

Ex. 88.

It results in a quite normal Baroque harmonic-melodic procedure. Compare, for example, its amended form with the answer in Ex. 74 on p. 64 from Murschhauser.

Even more to this particular point (although this means looking a little ahead) is Ex. 99b and 99c from Bach and Krebs respectively (p. 88), where we see the reiterated tonic-triad opening of their somewhat similarly constructed subjects being accorded both tonal and real replies within the space of a couple of bars.

A further questionable point in this theory concerns the terms 'tonic-triad', and 'tonic harmony', for can it be claimed for example that Bach's 'short' G minor subject opens with 'notes of the tonic triad', when in point of fact, Bach never once associates the second note of either subject or answer with tonic harmony? Exactly the same might be asked of Purcell's *Canzona*, Ex. 80b, on p. 68. Also, is Prout correct in saying that the subject from *Tolomeo* (Ex. 89) 'begins with the notes of the tonic chord'? In single-line melody yes, but hardly in its harmonized context:

Ex. 89. HANDEL, TOLOMEO

Ex. 90a, 90b, 90c, and 90d (all quoted by Prout in support of his theory) are a different matter entirely:

Ex. 90A.　Handel, Organ Concerto, No. 9 in B flat

Ex. 90B.　J. S. Bach, Clavier Sonata in D

Ex. 90C.　J. S. Bach, Cantata, Es ist dir gesagt

Ex. 90D.　J. S. Bach, Cantata, Bringet dem Herrn Ehre seines Namens

But even here, and this may appear a provocative attempt to develop an argument on the lines of the 'chicken or the egg', it is not a matter of dominant harmony *consciously*

answering tonic harmony, but of the answer reproducing in unmodified form, the melodic and harmonic pattern of the subject. If we admit to the former explanation (the conscious answering of tonic by dominant harmony) then we are recognizing the validity of Prout's tonic-triad theory; and if we recognize that, we must attempt all over again to account for the many tonal answers that have been quoted as proof against its validity. These considerations apart, it is questionable whether Bach would have modified the melodic line of Ex. 90d to Ex. 91, for the sake of tonal answer:

Ex. 91.

More evidence in support of these contentions will be produced in the next chapter, but for the moment it is hoped that sufficient proof has already been advanced to convince that the type of subject under discussion was regarded no differently from the type that opens with a direct leap from the tonic to its fifth; that a tonal answer in such cases constituted normal procedure, and not the reverse as Prout and others would have it, and that exceptions to this (i.e. the *real* answer) were the specific outcome of such factors as harmonic implications, and melodic line. Whereas the writer's theory endeavours to account satisfactorily for both tonal and real answers to subjects of this type, Prout leaves the former type without any satisfactory explanation.

CHAPTER IV

SUBJECTS COMMENCING ON THE DOMINANT

1. *RENAISSANCE PRACTICE*

It has already been pointed out that a tonal reply to 'subjects' opening with a leap from tonic to dominant was not a strict Renaissance procedure. It was, however, a different matter when a work commenced on the mode's dominant, for a re-examination of Palestrina's work with this aspect in mind, showed that an opening dominant would be responded to almost invariably by the same mode's final. Exceptions in Palestrina are comparatively so few, as to suggest that he himself regarded this procedure as a relatively strict one. These departures from his normal method of reply readily explain themselves. One case in point is the opening of his mass *O Regem Coeli* (transposed Dorian):

Ex. 92. PALESTRINA, MASS, O REGEM COELI

The real response to the initial dominant (D) probably arises from Palestrina's wish to preserve intact the opening figure (a) which serves as a thematic 'cell' for all the main portions of the Mass: *Kyrie I, Gloria, Credo, Sanctus,* and *Agnus Dei I* all open with this same 'subject'. Also, a real answer commencing on the mode's final would have involved using an A flat, which exceeded the allowable two flats of Musica Ficta.

Another exception is from the same composer's five-part motet *Vergine Saggia* (Hypo-Dorian mode). As with the preceding example, the mode's dominant (A) is not replied to by its final (D):

Ex. 93. PALESTRINA, MOTET, VERGINE SAGGIA

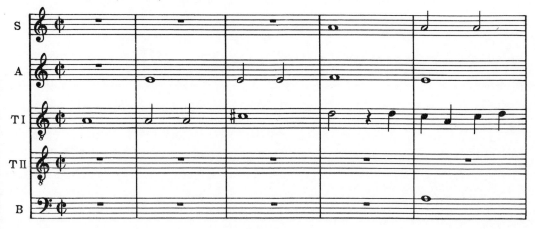

79

The following passage from Ernst Kurth's *Grundlagen des linearen Kontrapunkts* is illuminating because of its specific reference to the Palestrinian style, and because of its relevance to this particular texture:

'The inner dissolution of the linear foundation is shown in the weakening of the melodic independence of the voices. Their melodic treatment is more and more determined by the harmonic element; the lines adjust themselves to the progression of the chordal structure . . . and the melodic effects, especially of the middle parts, are absorbed by harmonic effects.'[1]

Here the initial 'E' of the 'answer' in alto and tenor II is, to borrow Kurth's phrase, 'determined by the harmonic element', which in this case is far closer to our D minor, than to Dorian tonality. This example is of exceptional interest, particularly in view of certain Baroque 'irregular' answers that stem from the same cause. Ex. 93 is of course, a relatively isolated example of its kind, but it plants, as it were, the seed of the Baroque 'irregular' answer, for we see the later period's normal practice of answering an initial dominant by tonic also yielding at times to the harmonic element.

These examples are quoted to demonstrate that Palestrina's comparatively rare departures from his normal practice of replying to dominant by final were not made without justification. The same may be claimed of Baroque practice in general.

In Renaissance practice, once the initial dominant had been answered by the mode's final, the answer either completed itself at subdominant level of pitch, or (less frequently) adjusted itself to normal dominant level. Exx. 94 and 95 show both procedures:

Ex. 94. PALESTRINA, MASS, VENI SPONSA CHRISTI

[1] Quoted from Jeppeson's *Counterpoint*, p. xi.

Ex. 95. Byrd, Motet, Ab ortu solis

One final point. Although it may sound a contradiction in terms, another way of looking at, say, Ex. 94, is that it opens with the *answer*, which is replied to by the *subject*. A Baroque parallel that comes to mind is the fugal section of the opening movement of Bach's third orchestral Suite in D.

2. BAROQUE PRACTICE

It is interesting to see certain aspects of Renaissance practice becoming reversed in the Baroque; a tonally answered subject now becomes the normal method of reply,[2] and a wholly subdominant one becomes what we might almost describe as abnormal. The reason for this is that whereas the Renaissance answer, whether at the fourth or fifth, leaves the tonality of the mode undisturbed, the Baroque answer coincides more often than not with a change of key; a dominant answer was preferred to a subdominant one because of the latter key's relatively subordinate position in their tonal designs. Even so, the Baroque attitude towards subjects commencing on the dominant was no less orderly than that of the Renaissance.

Prout comments, 'We now have to consider an important class of subjects—those that commence on the dominant. The old rule again was here absolute—that when the subject began on the dominant the answer must begin on the tonic. This rule, like that discussed in paras. 86 and 87, is observed by the great masters in the large majority of instances; but numerous exceptions are to be found to it.'[3] Later he adds,

We have given quite enough examples to prove that the rule as to answering dominant by tonic at the commencement of a subject is by no means so 'absolute' as it is declared to be by many theorists. For this there are two reasons. First there is the general principle . . . that tonic harmony in the subject should be replied to by dominant harmony in the answer. . . . Besides this, the melodic form of the subject should be kept unchanged as far as possible; and it is quite evident that in many cases the great composers felt this to be of much more importance than the keeping of an old rule which was made before modern tonality was established.

A further proof that but little weight was attached to the necessity for a tonal answer is found in the fact that sometimes in the first exposition of a fugue the first answer will be tonal and the second real . . .[4]

He concludes, 'The old theorists mostly follow one another blindly, like a flock of sheep through a hedge; and examiners in general adhere to the musty rules of two hundred years ago, taking little or no account of the progress made by music since that time.'[5]

These statements are hardly accurate. First, 'the musty rules of two hundred years ago' take us back in point of time[6] to the liberal interpretation of the tonal answer by such musicians as Purcell and Rameau. Secondly, Baroque practice suggests that Prout is

[2] See p. 19.
[3] *Fugue*, p. 41, para. 102.
[4] p. 46, para. 108.
[5] p. 48, para. 113.
[6] That is, from the year in which Prout's *Fugue* was first published (1891).

mistaken in asserting that in many cases real, in preference to tonal, answers were given because of the greater importance attached by composers to a subject's melodic shape. Here he is referring to subjects characterized by 'notes of the tonic chord', such as Ex. 86a on p. 75, whose authenticity, as we have just seen, is disproved by recent research. A number of subjects will be quoted later by way of disproving his assertion. Finally, his statement, 'A further proof that but little weight was attached to the necessity for a tonal answer is found in the fact that sometimes in the first exposition of a fugue the first answer will be tonal and the second real' could be misleading in that it implies an attitude of indifference on the part of the composer as to whether a tonal answer be given or not.

As already suggested, the Baroque attitude towards subjects commencing on the dominant, was no less orderly than that of the Renaissance; and viewed against the background of the two types of subject already discussed,[7] the basic principle is the same—that provided neither harmonic nor melodic elements intervened, the tonal answer constituted normal procedure. This principle is clearly illustrated in Ex. 96.

Ex. 96. BUXTEHUDE, MAGNIFICAT PRIMI TONI

---

[7] Those opening with a leap from tonic to dominant, or passing through the third of the scale.

The movement is founded upon two subjects (a), and (b).

(a) is modified in bar three to avoid making a V^6_4 chord[8]. The first answer to subject (a) (bar six) is tonal, but the next (bar eight) is real. The reason is plain; a tonal answer here would have meant the bass entering with the unprepared seventh of a V^4_2 chord—a technical feature not to be found in Buxtehude's work. In bar ten (a) and (b) are inverted. First there are two appearances of both subjects in bars ten and twelve. Two answers follow (bars fifteen and seventeen), and the harmonies permit (a) to be answered tonally on both occasions. So that we see a regularity of behaviour throughout, with subject (a)

---

[8] See f.n. 33 on p. 55.

consistently replied to tonally, except on the one occasion when the answer's course is determined by the harmonic element.

The reason advanced to account for Buxtehude's one real answer finds support in Bach's A major Organ Fugue, Ex. 97a. This work is the one quoted by Prout in support of his assertion 'but little weight was attached to the necessity for a tonal answer'.

Ex. 97A.   J. S. BACH, ORGAN PRELUDE AND FUGUE IN A

Bach's choice of harmonies for the first two notes of the answer's second entry (bar 33) rules out the possibility of tonal reply.

A tonal reply at the answer's second entry in Bach's G major Organ Fugue (Ex. 97b) would have created an impossible harmonic situation (impossible that is for the period), hence the real reply:

Ex. 97B.   J. S. Bach, Organ Prelude and Fugue in G

In the bass entry of the same composer's E major Organ Fugue on the other hand, the harmonies allow a tonal answer:

Ex. 97C.   J. S. Bach, Organ Toccata in E

Various melodic formulae. Three different melodic formulae, all commencing on the dominant, are now considered separately.

(i)   Subjects that open with a direct leap from dominant to tonic, or in which dominant and tonic are in relatively close proximity.[9]

(ii)   Subjects that open with 'notes of the tonic chord', either in direct, or indirect order.[10]

(iii)   Cases other than the above.[11]

In the Baroque, once a subject's initial dominant note had been replied to tonally, the answer generally adjusted itself to normal dominant level where it remained for the rest of its course.[12] Far more rarely, it completed itself at subdominant level throughout. This aspect is discussed in the next chapter.

It has been suggested that Baroque behaviour regarding subjects that commence on the dominant is no different from that applied to those that open with a leap from tonic to dominant, or those that pass through the tonic triad. So that with no new principles involved, it remains only to examine certain 'irregular' answers, drawn mainly from those quoted by Prout.

(i) Subjects that open with a leap from dominant to tonic.
Prout quotes the following, from Handel:

Ex. 98A.   HANDEL, ANTHEM, O COME LET US SING

---

[9] e.g., Book I, Nos. 13, 16, 21; Book II, Nos. 1, 2, 12.
[10] e.g., Book I, Nos. 3, 7, 24; Book II, Nos. 14, 15, 24.
[11] e.g., Book I, Nos. 11, 12; Book II, Nos. 16, 17, 20.
[12] The process may be seen in the majority of the 'Forty-Eight' quoted in f.n., 9–11 on this page.

Both examples are here quoted in full context. Both answers are 'caught up', as it were, in the move towards the dominant key ('absorbed by harmonic effects'), so that their real form is determined by the general harmonic context.

What Prout omits to point out is that the first answer in Ex. 98a *is* a tonal one, the first violins replying tonally to the subject in oboe and second violins. The situation in both these examples is thus the same as that in the fifth bar of Ex. 20b (p. 24) from *Messiah*.

(ii) Subjects that open with notes of the tonic chord, commencing on the dominant.

The type of subject commencing on the tonic with 'notes of the tonic chord' was dealt with in the previous chapter. All that was said regarding its misunderstanding by modern theory, Baroque procedure, and its effect upon tonality, applies equally here; (ii), therefore is no more than a variant of the subject that opens with a direct leap from dominant to tonic. Apart from commenting upon musical examples, little more remains to be said.

Prout writes, 'Our first group will be answers to subjects which commence with the notes of the tonic chord. . . . These are parallel cases to those given in paras. 94-99. [i.e. those that commence on the tonic.] In all of them the subject begins with tonic harmony and the answer replies with dominant harmony.'[13] By omitting to quote even one case of a tonally answered subject of this type, he must have led many an unwary student into accepting the real, rather than the tonal answer to such subjects as constituting normal Baroque procedure. His omission is not easy to understand, for with no difficulty at all it is possible to produce innumerable examples of tonal answers, whose weight of numbers alone, even if not establishing that they and not the real answer constitute normal procedure, at least weakens his case. So we commence by quoting a substantial group of tonally answered subjects, which together with the group quoted in the previous chapter (Ex. 82, pp. 70-72), constitutes a strong challenge as to the validity of the 'tonic triad' theory:

[13] *Fugue*, pp. 42–43, para. 105.

Ex. 99A. HANDEL, CONCERTO GROSSO, OP. 6, NO. 9 IN F

Ex. 99B. J. S. BACH, CLAVIER TOCCATA IN C MINOR

Ex. 99C. KREBS, FROM A. W. MARCHANT'S FUGUE SUBJECTS AND ANSWERS

Ex. 99D. ARNE, CONCERTO NO. 6 IN B FLAT

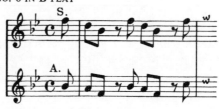

Ex. 99E. J. G. WALTHER, ORGAN FUGUE IN F

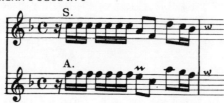

Ex. 99F. ALBRECHTSBERGER, FUGUE IN B FLAT

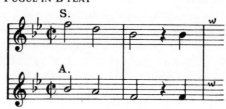

Ex. 99G. EBERLIN, FUGUE IN G

Ex. 99H. HANDEL, CHANDOS TE DEUM

Ex. 99I. BUXTEHUDE, ORGAN PRELUDE AND FUGUE IN A

Ex. 99J. J. S. BACH, CANTATA, ICH HATTE VIEL BEKÜMMERNIS

Ex. 99K. HANDEL, CLAVIER FUGUE IN G

Ex. 99L. MENDELSSOHN, FROM A. W. MARCHANT'S FUGUE SUBJECTS AND ANSWERS

Ex. 99M.   GRAUN, FROM A. W. MARCHANT'S FUGUE SUBJECTS AND ANSWERS

Ex. 99N.   MARPURG, FROM A. W. MARCHANT'S FUGUE SUBJECTS AND ANSWERS

Ex. 99O.   KUHNAU, FROM A. W. MARCHANT'S FUGUE SUBJECTS AND ANSWERS

Ex. 99P.   HANDEL, FROM A. W. MARCHANT'S FUGUE SUBJECTS AND ANSWERS

Ex. 99Q.   HANDEL, FROM A. W. MARCHANT'S FUGUE SUBJECTS AND ANSWERS

Ex. 99R.   FRESCOBALDI, CANZONA

Ex. 99s. HANDEL, WATER MUSIC

(See also Exx. 97b, 97c on p. 85, 167 on pp. 172–3, and Book I, Nos. 3, 7, 24; Book II, Nos. 2, 14, 15, 24. More could be added.)

Four examples from the group quoted by Prout are given in Ex. 100a, 100c, 100d, and 100f. Seen in full context, the various reasons accounting for the real form of their respective answers become clear. They have nothing to do with the tonic chord theory.

Ex. 100A. HANDEL, CONCERTO GROSSO, OP. 3, NO. 4 IN F

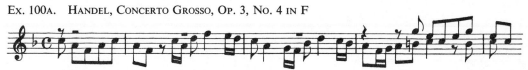

Ex. 100a shows the Chrysander version of subject and answer from Handel's fourth Concerto Grosso of Op. 3 which is the version quoted by Prout. However, the authoritative Bärenreiter edition[14] shows Handel using not a real, but a *tonal* reply at this point, and real replies at both viola and bass entries:

Ex. 100B. IBID.

Although Handel's tonal reply weakens Prout's case, paradoxically, the two real replies that follow ('notes of the tonic chord' notwithstanding) weaken it still further; for again, we may ask, is it likely that Handel would adhere to both 'the old rule', and to the 'higher and more important law' within the same exposition?

[14] H.H.-A. *Sechs Concerti Grossi*, Op. 3, ed. F. Hudson, Kassel, 1959, pp. 65–66. Refer also companion *Kritischer Bericht*, p. 93. (See also, p. 75.)

The reason behind this seeming irregularity is that whereas the local harmonic situation permits a tonal answer at the point of Violin I entry, it stands in the way of a similar response in the two answers that follow. The point of entry of both viola and bass coincides with some form of dominant harmony. An attempted tonal reply at the viola entry would result in VII$^6_4$, producing a situation identical with those already met with in Exx. 29, bar fifty-one (p. 29), 64b (p. 58), and 85d, bar nine (p. 74).

That these three composers should display identical behaviour within four identical situations is too significant to be dismissed as mere coincidence.

An attempted tonal reply at the bass entry of Ex. 100b would result in a harmonic combination as chaotic (for the period) as those resulting from attempted tonal replies in the C minor Organ Passacaglia (Ex. 72 bar six, p. 64), and in the Cantata *Gottes Zeit ist die allerbeste Zeit* (Ex. 101b, bar three). The behaviour in these contextually similar situations again is too consistent to be simple coincidence.

Ex. 100c.   J. S. Bach, Christmas Oratorio

The ending of subject and commencement of answer in Ex. 100c overlap, so that the latter is not a free agent in the matter of deciding its own form, which grows out of the prevailing harmony.

Ex. 100D.   HANDEL, ANTHEM, LET GOD ARISE

Similar circumstances account for the real answer in Ex. 100d.   Identical in the melodic formula of its opening, is the subject from the same composer's Concerto Grosso Op. 6, No. 2 in F (Ex. 100e), but here the clear-cut entry of the answer, free from complexities of overlapping, allows a tonal reply:

Ex. 100E.   HANDEL, CONCERTO GROSSO, OP. 6, NO. 2 IN F

Schumann's real answer is self-explanatory:

Ex. 100F.   SCHUMANN, PARADISE AND THE PERI

(*iii*) *Cases other than* (*i*) *and* (*ii*).
Three examples from the group quoted by Prout are given:

Ex. 101A. J. S. BACH, CLAVIER FUGUE IN A

    With the exposition in full, we can see the reason behind the real answer in bar three; it takes its form from an implied half-close in the tonic key. It also shows that by being 'moved a beat to the right' (i.e. to coincide with the chord of resolution in a V-I cadence),

94

the second and third appearances of the answer (bars ten and twelve) can now be replied to tonally. Prout omits to point this out.

Ex. 101B. J. S. Bach, Cantata, Gottes Zeit ist die allerbeste Zeit

Clearly, a tonal answer in the soprano entry of Ex. 101b is out of the question. In the bass entry, the thirteenth (of V) is no longer present, but an attempted tonal reply would mean that voice entering with the unprepared seventh of V_2^4. This is consistent with the many similar examples already met with.

Ex. 101C. J. S. Bach, Clavier Fantasia and Fugue in C minor

Seen in full context, the question arises, did Bach think of the opening notes of his subject as belonging to C minor at all? The entries in bars five and seventeen show that they set out on their tortuous harmonic routes not in C minor, but in A flat major, and the first entry of the answer (bar three) in its dominant, E flat major. Indeed, it is not until the subject's third entry in bar twenty-one that Bach identifies its opening notes with the key of C minor. This being so, the question of tonal answer does not arise. These considerations apart, the answer's initial note at its first appearance in bar three has no harmonic significance whatsoever.

This final example of a real reply is given in order to strengthen the writer's theory relating to the interaction between dominant harmony and the form of an answer:

Ex. 102.   LOEILLET, SONATA FOR RECORDER OBOE AND CONTINUO IN C MINOR

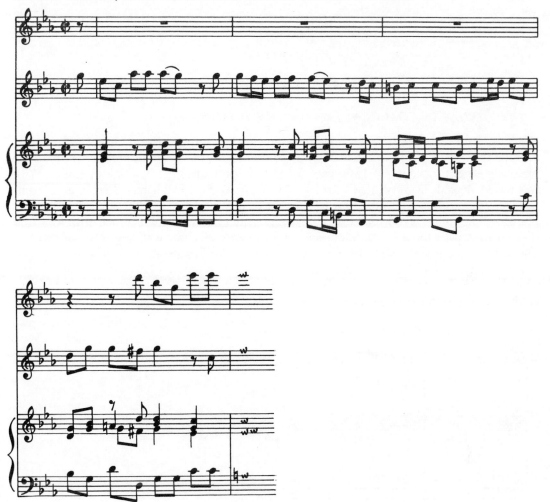

It is in company with Bach's 'short' G minor and G major Organ Fugues, Ex. 70 from Pachelbel (p. 62), Purcell's *Canzona* (Ex. 80b, p. 68), and others in this same group.

CHAPTER V

SUBDOMINANT ANSWERS

1. TO SUBJECTS COMMENCING ON THE DOMINANT

We have seen that Renaissance and Baroque practice met on common ground in their attitude towards subjects commencing on the dominant, in that both periods adopted the relatively strict procedure of answering the initial dominant note by final, or tonic. With this note satisfied, however, their respective ways parted, for whereas Renaissance composers were mostly content to allow the answer to complete itself at the same level of pitch (i.e. at subdominant level), Baroque composers were consciously concerned with avoiding this, so that with them the subdominant answer was of comparatively rare occurrence. The explanation is not a difficult one. An answer in the Renaissance, at whatever level of pitch, would normally be accomplished within the same mode. This may be seen in the opening of Palestrina's madrigal, *Mentre ch'al mar* (Ex. 103) where the one tonality serves for subject and answer alike:

Ex. 103.   PALESTRINA, MADRIGAL, MENTRE CH'AL MAR

It will be noticed that the relative position of tones and semitones in the subject is not strictly reproduced in the answer. This of course plays its part in preserving the one common tonality. The Baroque answer, on the other hand, more frequently than not associates itself with a different key, usually the dominant. It has been suggested that the period's comparatively rare resort to the subdominant answer may be attributed to the relatively subordinate position occupied by the subdominant key in its formal designs. The Baroque fugal exposition is normally limited to the period's two main tonalities, tonic and dominant.

We have seen that the normal Baroque method of reply to a subject commencing on the dominant is to answer the first note tonally (i.e. at subdominant level) and the remainder at dominant level.[1] *It is only when a subject's melodic line does not present oppor-*

---

[1] For example, all but three of the seventeen subjects in the 'Forty-Eight' commencing on the dominant conform to this plan.

tunity for subsequent adjustment, or when it is necessary to redress tonal balance, that a subdominant answer is resorted to. This is illustrated in the group of subdominantly-answered subjects in Ex. 109a—109e, on pp. 100-1. Experiment will show that none of this group lends itself readily to melodic adjustment. Consider for a moment the openings of Ex. 104a and 104b:

Ex. 104A. J. S. Bach, Organ Fantasia and Fugue in G minor

Ex. 104B. J. S. Bach, Organ Toccata in D minor

Whereas the line of the former provides opportunity for melodic adjustment, the latter, by reason of its unbroken semiquaver movement, and the stepwise formation of its melody (short of repeating its initial note), does not; so that the former is answered tonally, and the latter subdominantly throughout. Let us experiment by interchanging their respective openings:

Ex. 105A.

Ex. 105B.

In its new guise, we may be tolerably certain that the reply to the D minor subject (Ex. 104b) would have been a tonal one, as in Ex. 106:

Ex. 106.

—for it is precisely thus that Bach answers the subject of the second of his *Eight Little Preludes and Fugues* (BWV 554), whose melodic outline in its opening few notes is identical with that of Ex. 104b:

Ex. 107. J. S. Bach, Eight Little Preludes and Fugues, No. 2 in D minor

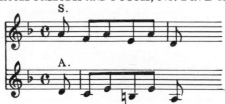

H

Conversely, in its new form, the answer to the G minor subject, whether at dominant or subdominant level must needs follow a real course throughout:

Ex. 108.

The two causes suggested for subdominant answers (unyielding melodic line, and redress of tonal balance) are now considered separately.

(i) Unyielding melodic line

Ex. 109A.   J. S. BACH, CLAVIER PARTITA IN B MINOR

Ex. 109B.   J. S. BACH, ORGAN PRELUDE AND FUGUE IN C

Ex. 109C.   PACHELBEL, FROM MARPURG'S ABHANDLUNG VON DER FUGUE

Ex. 109D.   SCHUMANN, FUGHETTA

Codetta

Ex. 109E. BEETHOVEN, QUARTET IN C SHARP MINOR, OP. 131

The replies to this entire group are subdominant answers in the true meaning of the word, in that they all touch upon the subdominant *key*, and remain at that level of pitch throughout. Only by this resort to subdominant reply can their respective initial dominant notes be replied to by tonic. It follows that if the answer be strict as in this group, subdominant tonality must inevitably result.

Although in a later answer Bach goes into the key of the subdominant, he avoids doing this during the entire exposition of his D minor 'Fiddle' fugue (Ex. 110), which remains in the tonic key throughout:

Ex. 110. J. S. BACH, ORGAN PRELUDE AND FUGUE IN D MINOR

In answering the subject of Ex. 110 on a different cross-section of the *same scale*, he thus comes nearer the Renaissance ideal of confining subject and answer within the same mode. Even so, I suggest that the subdominant answer, as with the group above, is resorted to because its melodic line offers no opportunity for effecting mutation.

(ii) *Tonal balance*

An answer at subdominant level (not necessarily in the subdominant *key*) is sometimes resorted to in order to achieve, or redress, tonal balance. Such a situation is not infrequently met with in the French Overture, when, as is often the case, a fugal section sets out in the complementary key of the movement.[2] An example that readily comes to mind is the first movement of Bach's F major Clavier Suite:

Ex. 111.   J. S. Bach, Clavier Suite in F

The first section, the normal slow introduction, ends in the complementary key of C major. The second section, a fugue, sets out in that key, and a subdominant answer (or perhaps we should say an answer at subdominant level of pitch) is given in order to achieve tonal balance between the two main tonalities, tonic and dominant. It presents a case entirely different from the group quoted in Ex. 109, whose answers are in the subdominant *key*. Indeed, it can hardly be termed a subdominant answer, for strictly speaking it is no more than a reversal of the normal entry order of subject and answer. It is in similar case to Ex. 94 on p. 80, for although a seeming contradiction in terms, the fugue could be regarded as opening with the *answer*, which is replied to by the *subject*.

This procedure is perhaps nowhere more clearly demonstrated than in an ingenious fugal *tour de force* by Krieger. He writes four separate fugues on different subjects, finally combining them in a quadruple fugue. The answer to the subject of Fugue I appears at first glance to be a subdominant one (Ex. 112a), but the initial pair of entries in the quadruple fugue (Ex. 112b) proves it to be no more than a reversal of the normal entry order of subject and answer, and not a subdominant answer after all:

Ex. 112A.   J. P. Krieger, Clavier Fugue in C

---

[2] The opening movement of Bach's first Orchestral Suite answers to this formal plan, but as the melodic line of the subject provides opportunity for tonal reply, the question of subdominant answer does not arise.

Ex. 112B.   IBID.

A further subdominantly answered subject, in similar case to the F major Clavier Suite, is the second part of the Gigue in Bach's sixth *English Suite:*

Ex. 113.   J. S. Bach, English Suite, No. 6

and the subdominant answers in Bach's third orchestral *Suite* (Ex. 114a), and Cantata No. 34 (Ex. 114b), although touching upon the subdominant key, arise from the same cause. Observe the similarity of melodic line and tonal design in Ex. 114a and 114b:

Ex. 114A.   J. S. Bach, Suite for Orchestra, No. 3 in D

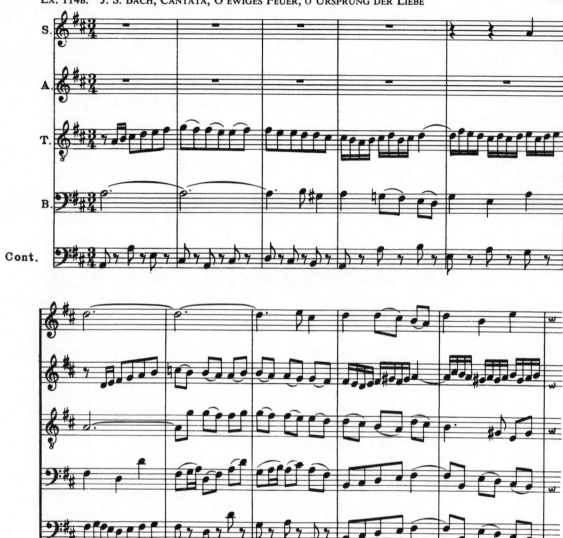

The subdominant answer in Bach's cantata, *Herr, deine Augen* is the effect of a some-what different aspect of tonal design. Subject and answer are shown in full context:

Ex. 115A.   J. S. BACH, CANTATA, HERR, DEINE AUGEN

A first glance may suggest a real answer at the fifth (Ex. 115b) as being equally good, particularly in view of the fact that the subdominant key of C minor, with which the subject was ushered in, has now been left well behind:

Ex. 115B.

Another seemingly good reason for an answer at the fifth is that the subdominant key would be avoided. The reason against this solution, and therefore the reason accounting for the subdominant reply, is that an answer at the fifth would involve the supertonic key of A minor, in reply to the subject's modulation to D minor at the corresponding point. As already pointed out, the exposition of a fugue seldom goes outside the 'circle of fifths', tonic, dominant, and subdominant. It is therefore a further example of tonal stability being maintained by the expedient of subdominant reply.

It is for this same reason of tonal control that Bach deliberately *avoids* a subdominant answer in Ex. 116:

Ex. 116.   J. S. Bach, Chromatic Fantasia and Fugue in D minor

Two all-important factors here combine to suggest a subdominant answer as the only reasonable solution: (i) that the subject commences on the dominant, and (ii) that its chromatic scale-line appears to offer no opportunity for effecting mutation. Yet Bach *does* effect mutation, and *does* give other than a subdominant answer. He deliberately interrupts the chromatic line of his theme in order to *avoid* a subdominant reply, which in this case would lead the tonality into the remote key of C minor, in reply to the subject's modulation to G minor at the corresponding point. (Compare bars eleven, twelve, and thirteen of the answer with bars three, four, and five of the subject.)

Wider Aspects of Tonal Design

Until now discussion concerning the interaction of subdominant answer and tonal design has been confined to the exposition of a fugue. We round off this section by examining two examples in which the form of each answer is the outcome of, or determined by, a wider aspect of tonal design; in the one, of a complete movement, and in the other of a three-movement work. The prominence accorded dominant harmony in Ex. 117 plus the initial dominant note of Ex. 118a, and the unsympathetic response of both melodic lines to adjustment, all point to a subdominant answer in each case as the most reasonable and likely solution. Yet whereas the former is given one, the latter is not:

Ex. 117.   J. S. Bach, Cantata, Der Himmel lacht

The movement from which Ex. 117 is quoted is the first chorus in the cantata, whose central key is C major. The movement divides into four distinct sections; call them A^1, B, C, and A^2. A^1, forty-two bars in length, concludes with a strongly marked cadence in the complementary key of G major. Next follows B, a short adagio section of eight bars, which after passing through A minor and D minor ends, like A^1, in G major. C now follows, a short fugal section of twelve bars, based on the subject quoted in Ex. 117. A subdominant answer is insisted upon in reply to each of the subject's three entries, *so that the entire section confines itself to F major and C major.* A short ritornello in the orchestra follows (A^2) which completes the *formal* design by recapitulating the main theme, and the *tonal* design by re-establishing the tonic key of C major.

The incidence of subdominant answer in itself is of secondary importance. Its real significance is the role it plays in the tonal and architectural design of the movement *as a whole*—the subdominant section of a balanced and typically classical tonal pattern.

Ex. 118A.   J. S. Bach, Clavier Toccata in E minor

The order of precedence between the form of an answer and the wider aspect of tonal design is perhaps nowhere more clearly demonstrated than in Ex. 118a, whose subject is

106

answered, most unexpectedly, at the fifth. Concerning this subject and answer, Kitson makes the point that 'a tonal answer . . . would ruin its melodic curve'.[3]

Ex. 118ʙ.

Following in his wake, Oldroyd writes, of the same subject and answer, 'The application of this old custom of answering a subject dominantly at the outset served to avoid repeated notes at a conspicuous point. Thus the following by Bach.'[4] (His musical illustration is the same as Kitson's.)

Both Kitson and Oldroyd miss the point, surely, which, I suggest, has nothing to do with avoiding the repeated E's at all, for sufficient examples of 'repeated notes at a conspicuous point' have already been quoted (Exx. 34a—34c, on p. 34, and 35a—35e, on pp. 34–35) to suggest that this is not necessarily the reason behind Bach's unexpected answer. It is unlikely that the version they both reject (Ex. 118b) would have occurred to Bach in any case. Both Kitson and Oldroyd appear to overlook the fact that because the subject commences on the dominant, and because its melodic line offers no opportunity for tonal reply, instinctively one looks for a straightout subdominant answer, such as Handel gives to a subject whose opening is identical:[5]

Ex. 119. HANDEL, CAPRICCIO FOR CLAVIER IN G

The truth is that the reason for Bach's seemingly irregular behaviour in not answering his subject subdominantly becomes apparent only by examining the part in relation to the whole.

The fugue is the final movement of the Toccata. The first movement (an introduction and double fugue) is mainly in the tonic key of E minor, and its dominant, B minor. The second movement, an adagio, has a strong subdominant bias. After this, a firmly established tonic key for the final movement becomes imperative; and so we see all nine entries of the theme confining themselves exclusively to the keys of tonic and dominant for subject and answer respectively. Moreover, apart from brief passing references to related keys, the fugue as a whole is centred around these two main tonalities. Had the fugue stood as an isolated movement, then it is quite conceivable that, as in the Handel example, a subdominant answer might have been given. But having regard to the fugue's position in the work's overall formal design, and bearing in mind the strong subdominant bias of the

[3] *Fugal Construction*, p. 20.
[4] *Technique and Spirit*, p. 78.
[5] But see how Handel adroitly avoids the subdominant *key* by answering C natural in each case by F sharp.

movement which precedes it, the tonic-dominant tonality of the fugue itself appears the only reasonable solution, and incidentally the only apparent reason for the answer given.

2. TO SUBJECTS COMMENCING ON OTHER THAN THE DOMINANT

Ex. 120. J. S. BACH, THE ART OF FUGUE, CONTRAPUNCTUS X

This subject's somewhat unusual structure—the initial leading note,[6] the characteristic (and profoundly beautiful) rise of the sixth, together with the prominence accorded the two soundings of the dominant note—does not lend itself readily to melodic adjustment. Thus the subdominant answer is given, presumably, in order to satisfy the two prominently-placed dominant notes. The tonal balance is redressed with the next pair of entries (in which subject and answer become inverted), which follow in the normal order of tonic and dominant.

3. PROUT'S THEORY

To the writer, Prout's theory concerning the subdominant answer is not easy to understand. After quoting subject and answer (among others) of Exx. 109b (p. 100), 117 (p. 106), and 121

Ex. 121. MENDELSSOHN, SURREXIT PASTOR

he comments, 'If we examine the three subjects last given, we shall see that in all of them prominence is given to the dominant or to notes of the dominant harmony.'[7] So far so good. He then quotes subject and answer of the B minor Clavier Fugue (Ex. 109a, p. 100), analyzing it thus: 'Here the subject commences with the arpeggio of the dominant seventh; then comes tonic harmony, and then dominant harmony again. The answer is now in the subdominant, in order to carry out the important principle that dominant harmony should be answered by tonic.'[8]

---

[6] It will be recalled that the subject of Book II, No. 13 in F sharp major which also begins on the leading-note, has a subdominant colouring.

[7] *Fugue*, pp. 26–27, para. 72.

[8] p. 27, para. 72.

Here we meet with the first difficulty. His analysis is self-contradictory, for after admitting the answer to be in the *subdominant*, he then reasons that the dominant harmony in the subject is balanced by *tonic* harmony in the answer! Yet it is quite plain from the text that V in B minor in the subject is balanced by V in E minor in the answer.

Other examples he quotes are the subjects and answers of the D minor 'Fiddle' fugue (Ex. 110, p. 101) and the D minor Organ Toccata fugue (Ex. 104b, p. 99). He remarks, 'Our next illustrations . . . further show the answering of dominant harmony at the commencement of the subject by tonic harmony at the beginning of the answer.'[9] It has been pointed out that the exposition of Ex. 110 remains in the tonic key throughout. Its subdominant answer, therefore, is not a matter of answering dominant harmony, but of satisfying the subject's initial dominant note. Ex. 104b is in no different case from Ex. 109a, in that tonic tonality in the subject is balanced not by *tonic*, but by subdominant tonality in the answer.

Of Ex. 114a, on p. 103, Prout writes, 'The subject, except the last note, is formed entirely of dominant harmony, which is therefore answered by corresponding tonic harmony. The counterpoint accompanying the answer conclusively proves the key of the answer to be G.'[10] How can it be reasoned that dominant harmony in the subject is balanced by tonic harmony in the answer, when as he himself points out, the accompanying counterpoint proves it to be in the key of G? As suggested on p. 81, because the fugue sets out from the complementary key (A), the process here could be viewed not so much as a subdominantly answered subject, as a reversal of the normal entry order of subject and answer; thus we could regard the fugue as leading off with the *answer*, which is replied to by the *subject*.

Prout rounds off by quoting, among others, Ex. 122 from Handel's *Solomon*, and Ex. 109e on p. 101 from Beethoven's C sharp minor Quartet (Op. 131) with the comment, 'We now add a few examples, by other composers, of real answers in the subdominant key.'[11] His rule in summary is, 'Whenever, in a subject which ends in the key of the tonic, particular prominence is given to dominant harmony, especially near the beginning of the subject, the answer may be in the subdominant key, in order to conform to the important general principle that dominant harmony in the subject should be replied to by tonic harmony in the answer.'[12]

Ex. 122. HANDEL, SOLOMON

[9] pp. 28–29, para. 76.
[10] pp. 29–30, para. 78.
[11] p. 30, para. 79.
[12] pp. 30–31, para. 80.

The point that puzzles is that after drawing attention repeatedly to the subdominant key of the many answers he quotes, he follows with a contradictory statement by referring to this same *subdominant* harmony as *tonic* harmony. We are given a clue to his reasoning in his analysis of the subject and answer of Bach's cantata *Herr, deine Augen:* (See Ex. 115a, on pp. 104-5.)

Here the subject does not, like those previously given, begin with a note of the dominant chord; but the diminished fifth immediately following clearly indicates the chord of the dominant seventh. . . . This choice of a key [C minor] for the answer enables Bach to carry out the important general principle already mentioned . . . that dominant harmony in the subject should be replied to by tonic harmony in the answer. Here we have the *dominant* seventh chord in G at the first bar of the subject, answered by the notes of the *tonic* seventh of G in the first bar of the answer. It would have been quite possible to give a real answer for this bar, beginning on the dominant; but then the dominant harmony of the subject would have been answered by the supertonic harmony, [13] instead of the tonic.[14]

From his analysis, it now emerges that by 'tonic harmony' Prout means tonic *chromatic* harmony. Re-examining, say, Ex. 109a on p. 100 in this light, Prout's reasoning is that the dominant seventh chord of B minor in the subject is replied to by the tonic chromatic seventh chord at the corresponding point in the answer. Unfortunately, he destroys his case by his own rule concerning the use of the tonic chromatic seventh chord: 'The tonic seventh so strongly suggests the subdominant key that special care is needed to contradict the suggestion in its resolution. The practice of the great composers is therefore to resolve the chord either on a dominant or on a supertonic *discord* in the same key, the former being the more common.'[15]

According to his own rule therefore, none of the examples he cites are true tonic sevenths, but dominant seventh chords in the key of the subdominant.

Theoretical wrangling apart, to the ear the tonic chord and the tonic chromatic seventh chord, especially in a minor key, have little in common beyond the word 'tonic'. No amount of theoretical argument will convince the ear that apart from Exx. 110 and 122, the answers quoted by Prout are in other than the key of the subdominant; and no line of reasoning can convince the ear that subdominant key equals tonic key. Indeed, the only true example he quotes of 'tonic harmony answering dominant harmony' is that from *Solomon* (Ex. 122), in which V, bar one of the subject is answered by I at the corresponding point in the answer.

We return to *Herr, deine Augen* (Ex. 115a) to see this theory overreaching itself. Prout writes: 'It will also be seen that at the second bar of the subject there is a modulation to the dominant key. Such a modulation is almost invariably answered by a return to the tonic key. Here, however, the tonic harmony in the answer is really the harmony of the dominant of C minor.'[16] The full text of this work shows the B natural in the second bar of the answer as part of a diminished seventh chord, B natural, F, A flat; the claim that this should be regarded simultaneously as *tonic* harmony in G minor, and *dominant* harmony in C minor is not easy to accept.

This unnecessary complication is created of course, by Prout's odd refusal to acknowledge openly the presence of a third tonality—that of the subdominant. This is mentioned here because Prout's line of reasoning forms the basis of both his and others' method of analysis which they apply to one particular type of modulating subject. This is discussed in the chapter that follows.

[13] Why not call it what it is, dominant harmony in D minor in response to dominant harmony in G minor?
[14] pp. 27–28, paras. 73–74.
[15] E. Prout, *Harmony: Its Theory and Practice*, 16th ed., London, 1901, p. 220, para. 496.
[16] *Fugue*, p. 28, para. 75.

110

4. PARTIAL SUBDOMINANT ANSWERS

The answer to a subject that opens with tonic and dominant notes in relatively close proximity, is normally adjusted to dominant level, once the conditions of tonal reply have been met. In the 'Forty-Eight', for example, all seven subjects that open in this manner (Book I, Nos. 2, 8, 17, 22, and Book II, Nos. 3, 7, and 11) answer to this plan. It sometimes happens however, that a subject's melodic line does not lend itself to subsequent adjustment. In this case, the answer, after replying to the subject's initial note at the fifth, generally completes itself at subdominant level, though not necessarily in the subdominant *key*. Consider Ex. 123a—123d:

Ex. 123A. BUXTEHUDE, ORGAN PRELUDE AND FUGUE IN A MINOR

Ex. 123B. BUXTEHUDE, ORGAN PRELUDE AND FUGUE IN G MINOR

Ex. 123C. J. S. BACH, CLAVIER PRELUDE AND FUGUE IN E FLAT

Structurally, they have one feature in common—a conjunct melodic line—and it is this, I suggest, that stands in the way of subsequent adjustment to the fifth. The problem becomes even more acute in the case of the two chromatic subjects from Bach.

Remarkable in its tonal design is the G minor fugue (Ex. 123b), where, apart from that implied in bar three, cadences are neatly avoided until the very end of the exposition. It is a classic contradiction of the average textbook's assertion that the answer is a reproduction of the subject in a different *key*. Although answering his subject at subdominant *pitch*, Buxtehude avoids the subdominant *key*, so that throughout the exposition, and indeed the ensuing counter-exposition, subject and answer remain in the tonic.

CHAPTER VI

MODULATING SUBJECTS

1. *PRELIMINARIES*

The gulf that divides theory from practice in the matter of the modulating subject is a wide one. This gulf is the direct result of an arbitrary rule, indiscriminately applied by theory to all modulating subjects alike, but having no foundation in actual practice. This rule is quoted later in the chapter. Before setting out therefore to examine the modulating subject according to theory, it is necessary to arrive at a suitable basis for discussion.

The generally accepted meaning of the term 'modulating subject' is that it is one which ends in a different key (usually the dominant) from that in which it set out. We should differentiate between the true modulating subject and one that is taken to the dominant key by means of a codetta. An example of the latter is the 'short' G minor Organ Fugue (Ex. 50b, p. 47). The subject proper ends on the third beat of the fifth bar in the tonic key, and is then taken to D minor by means of a codetta. That it is a codetta, and not an integral part of the subject itself, is proved by the fact that it drops out of the fugue completely after the first three exposition entries. True modulating subjects are relatively few. In the 'Forty-Eight' for example, there are only four: Book I, Nos. 7, 10, 18, and 24. Certain others, such as Book II, Nos. 10 and 15 are taken to the dominant by means of a codetta.

The modulating subject poses two problems peculiar to itself; they concern structure, and tonality.

2. *STRUCTURE*

As the tonalities of a fugal exposition are usually limited to tonic, dominant, and (more rarely) subdominant keys, it follows that a modulating subject must be replied to tonally if it is to be contained within these limits. For example, a real answer at the fifth throughout to the subject of Book I, No. 7 in E flat would end in the key of its supertonic, F major. One difficulty encountered in the answering of a modulating subject is that of having to decide just where mutation is best effected. In this particular example, Bach effects mutation following the rest, so that from this point to the end, the subject is replied to at subdominant level, thus making possible an ending in the tonic key. In this case the rest marks the obvious point at which mutation is best effected; but many other subjects are not so obliging. However, we are helped by the fact that modulating subjects in general belong to one of three different structural patterns, which for convenience we group thus:

    (i)   Those whose melodic line is marked by a division.
    (ii) Those with an 'indivisible' or 'unyielding' melodic line.
    (iii) Those whose opening is marked with prominently placed tonic and dominant notes.

(i) The divisible type.

In this type, a distinct division in the subject is discernible through either a rest or a cadence, and mutation is effected immediately following this division. As no two subjects are necessarily alike in construction, it follows that there can be no generalization as to where mutation is likely to be effected; it may be early or late in the answer's course, according to its individual structure. The reason for this somewhat obvious comment becomes apparent later in the chapter.

Mutation following a rest. Book I, No. 7 in E flat has already been quoted. Other examples answering to this same structural pattern are Ex. 124, and Ex. 127c and 127d on pp. 128–30.

Ex. 124.   J. S. BACH, CLAVIER FUGUE IN A

The process is obvious. Further discussion is unnecessary.

Mutation following a cadence.

Ex. 125A.   J. S. BACH, CANTATA, SINGET DEM HERRN EIN NEUES LIED

S.

9 10 11 12

A.

T.

B.

Ex. 125B. J. S. Bach, Clavier Toccata in G

Ex. 125c. J. S. Bach, Three-part Inventions, No. 3 in D

Ex. 125d. Handel, Concerto Grosso, Alexander's Feast

Ex. 125E.   J. K. Kerll, Fugue in C

Ex. 125F.   Albrechtsberger, Fugue in E

Ex. 125G.   J. S. Bach, Capriccio for Clavier in B flat

Ex. 125H. ALBRECHTSBERGER, FUGUE IN F

Ex. 125I.   Mozart, Mass in F, K.192

Ex. 125J.   J. S. Bach, Organ Fantasia and Fugue in A minor

In bars two and three of the exposition of Ex. 125a, a V-I cadence in the tonic is immediately followed by a modulation to the dominant. A parallel V-I cadence in the dominant key occurs at the corresponding point of the answer (bars five and six), and mutation is effected immediately following the cadence, which in this particular example coincides with a return to the tonic, D major. (As we shall see, mutation and the return modulation to the tonic key do not, as in this instance, always coincide.) The process repeats itself in the second entries of subject and answer. (Compare bars eight and nine with eleven and twelve.) Ex. 125b, 125c, 125d, 125e, and 125f, follow a parallel process. In Ex. 125g the first implied cadence in bars three and four marks a modulation to the dominant, and mutation is effected immediately following a parallel cadence in C minor at the corresponding point of the answer (bar eight), so that although the modulatory scheme differs from others in the group, the actual principle involved is the same. Ex. 125h from Albrechtsberger is a parallel case. In Ex. 125i the cadence points in subject and answer do not exactly correspond, mutation occurring immediately following the return modulation to the tonic in bar nine, so that again the principle involved is the same. In Ex. 125j, A minor tonality is re-established, following incidental modulation, by means of a V-VI cadence in C (see bar thirteen), which is immediately followed by a modulation to the dominant. Conversely, the dominant key is re-established at the corresponding point in the answer by a parallel V-VI cadence in G in bar seven, following which mutation effects a return modulation to A minor.

Space does not permit the inclusion of further examples, but a sufficient number has been given to demonstrate the basic principle, that although mutation is apparent through the melody, it is the *harmony* that is the true determining factor, in that it creates the *opportunity* for mutation; in every case in Ex. 125 mutation follows closely upon a cadence.

(*ii*)   *The indivisible type.*

In this type, the subject is interrupted by neither cadence nor rest, and mutation is effected at the very outset of the answer's course by a process described a little later.

The two factors in Ex. 125 by which mutation is made possible, either a rest or a cadence, are absent from the examples that follow:

Ex. 126A.   BUXTEHUDE, ORGAN PRELUDE AND FUGUE IN C

Ex. 126B. J. S. Bach, Cantata, Gott ist mein König

Ex. 126C. J. S. Bach, Organ Prelude and Fugue in C

121

Ex. 126D.   J. S. Bach, 'Forty-Eight', Book I, No. 18

Ex. 126E.   J. S. Bach, St Matthew Passion

Ex. 126f. Pergolese, Organ Fugue in G

D: I = G V

D: I = G V

Ex. 126G.   HANDEL, ISRAEL IN EGYPT

E: I

A: V

Ex. 126H.   MOZART, MASS IN C, K.115

G: I=C: V

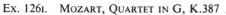

Ex. 126I. MOZART, QUARTET IN G, K.387

D: I = G V

Ex. 126J. PACHELBEL, CHORALE PRELUDE, O MENSCH, BEWEIN DEIN SÜNDE GROSS

C: I = F: V

125

Ex. 126K.   PURCELL, TEN SONATAS OF FOUR PARTS, No. 4

Ex. 126L.   J. S. BACH, MAGNIFICAT

A: I   D V

Ex. 126a–126l belongs to a different structural pattern, an unyielding melodic line; and the process of mutation likewise is dissimilar. In addition to the absence of rests and intermediate cadences, the problem of where to effect mutation is made no easier by such features as sequential patterns (126b and 126f), scalic and chromatic runs (126a and 126k), and characteristic intervals such as the augmented fourth in 126d, the diminished fourth and fifth in 126e, and the perfect fourth in 126i. Experiment will prove how very difficult it is to effect mutation satisfactorily at any point other than that chosen by the composers.

Thus modulating subjects answering to this particular structure possess characteristics that are closely similar to those of subjects accorded subdominant answers, of which it was remarked (pp. 98–99): *It is only when a subject's melodic line does not present opportunity for subsequent adjustment, or when it is necessary to redress tonal balance, that a subdominant answer is resorted to.*

It was suggested on pp. 113–14 when discussing the 'divisible' type of subject, that no generalization could be made as to where mutation was likely to occur in answers to subjects of that type; it might occur at an answer's beginning, middle, or end. But in this group, there emerges a uniform pattern of behaviour, for in every case mutation is effected at the very outset of the answer's course. This regularity of procedure points strongly to the presence of one fundamental principle governing answers of this particular structural pattern. *This principle, it is suggested, is that when mutation at any other point proves difficult, it is effected at the very outset of the answer's course, by utilizing the final harmony of the subject as a means of restoring tonic tonality.* Thus in Ex. 126a, 126b, 126c, 126f, 126i, 126j, and 126l, the final harmony in the subject is treated as pivotal (dominant key I equals tonic V) with the ♮7 not infrequently appearing as a passing note. Handel is able to make a return to tonic tonality in 126g, by the simple expedient of ending the subject with a *Tierce de Picardie.* (I equals V.)

♯

Although in this group the actual process of mutation is apparent through the melody, again it is the *harmony* that creates the opportunity, and thus determines the point at which mutation is to be effected. It is important to our later discussion that we should be clear upon this order of cause and effect.

(*iii*)   *Subjects whose opening is marked with prominently placed tonic and dominant notes.*
Answers to subjects in this group generally present no problem, for if answered tonally, whereby the fifth is exchanged for a fourth, a tonic ending is assured. The technique explains itself in Ex. 127a–127i:

Ex. 127A.   Buxtehude, Organ Prelude and Fugue in E minor

Ex. 127c.   J. S. Bach, Organ Toccata and Fugue in C

Ex. 127D. J. S. Bach, Cantata, Ich hatte viel Bekümmernis

Ex. 127E. PACHELBEL, CHORALE PRELUDE, WO GOTT ZUM HAUS NICHT GIBT SEIN GUNST

Ex. 127F. PACHELBEL, CHORALE PRELUDE, EIN FESTE BURG IST UNSER GOTT

K

Ex. 127H.   Handel, Hercules

Ex. 127i.   BEETHOVEN, FIFTEEN VARIATIONS WITH FUGUE, OP. 35

It is interesting to see in Ex. 127c and 127d how, once tonic and dominant notes have been replied to tonally, their answers are momentarily restored to dominant level, only to revert to subdominant level by a second mutation. Even so, and it is important to note this, tonic tonality remains virtually undisturbed throughout the answer's course in Ex. 127d, and very nearly so in Ex. 127c.

It might also be reasoned that in Ex. 127a—127g and 127i, the harmony exercises an equally important function in the process, for in each of these cases, the final harmony of the subject is treated as pivotal, dominant key I becoming tonic V. This is clearly the significance of the *Tierce de Picardie* in bar five of the E minor example from Buxtehude, Ex. 127a, and the strong evidence of ♮7 introduced as a passing note in others.

The three different structures have one further contrasting characteristic. Whereas in (i) mutation is effected immediately *following* a cadence, in (ii) and (iii) it is effected *within* a cadence.

3.   TONAL BALANCE BETWEEN SUBJECT AND ANSWER

Prout's rule is inflexible: 'If the subject begin in the tonic, and modulate to the dominant, the answer must begin in the dominant and modulate to the tonic. This important rule needs to be supplemented by another: The modulation in the answer from dominant back to tonic must be made at the same point at which the modulation was made in the subject from tonic to dominant.'[1] This is the damaging rule referred to at the commencement of the chapter. It is in line with a rule quoted earlier in the nineteenth century by writers including Cherubini[2] and Higgs,[3] and later reiterated by such writers as Gédalge,[4] Macpherson,[5] R. O. Morris,[6] and Bairstow.[7] This rule will be discussed later, but for the moment, it is sufficient to repeat that it has absolutely no foundation in practice.

If we re-examine Ex. 125a–125e on pp. 114–17, we find a group in which perfect symmetrical tonal balance is maintained between subject and answer, for in all five examples, the tonic and dominant sections of the subject are reversed proportionately in the answer. Symmetry is maintained in yet another way, for melodic and tonal adjustment are effected simultaneously. This group exemplifies perfectly the textbook rule.

[1] *Fugue*, pp. 49–50, paras. 116–7.
[2] *Counterpoint and Fugue*, p. 67.
[3] *Fugue*, p. 24, paras. 54–56.
[4] *Traité de la fugue*, pp. 12–13, paras. 25–30.
[5] *Counterpoint*, p. 103.
[6] R. O. Morris, *The Structure of Music*, London, 1935, p. 94.
[7] *Counterpoint and Harmony*, p. 317.

On the other hand, the textbook rule is badly upset in Ex. 126a–126c and 126f–126k on pp. 120–1 and 123–6, in that the point of modulation in the answer back to tonic does not correspond with the point of modulation in the subject away from tonic. Apart from the first note or two, each of these answers is in the tonic key throughout. Neither is the dominant key dwelt upon for any length of time in either Ex. 126d or 126e, whose answers make their return to the tonic key via the key of the subdominant. In similar case is the entire group of Ex. 127 on pp. 127–33, where apart from incidental, or transient, modulation (such as in Ex. 127c), the answers again, after the first note or two, are in the tonic key throughout. In this same connection, see Book I, No. 24, in which the answer is in the tonic key for the greater part of its course, and Book I, No. 7 (Ex. 128), in which the answer is wholly in the key of the tonic:

Ex. 128.   J. S. Bach, 'Forty-Eight', Book I, No. 7

From the two groups in Exx. 126 and 127, we see emerging two fundamentally important factors, both relating to tonal design. They are (contrary to most textbooks' rule on the matter) that an answer does not necessarily reproduce the same tonal balance as that of its subject; and that the points of tonal and melodic adjustment in the answer do not necessarily correspond. In the 'head-and-tail' type of modulating subject (i.e. one divided into two distinct parts by a rest) the rest generally marks the point of tonal division between tonic and dominant keys; but although the rest at the corresponding place in the answer may still mark the point of *melodic* adjustment, it does not necessarily mark the point of converse modulation from dominant back to tonic, for the two (melodic and tonal adjustment) are sometimes effected independently of each other. Thus, whereas the rest in bar one of Ex. 128 marks the point of *tonal* division in the subject, and *melodic* adjustment in the answer, the converse modulation from dominant back to tonic in the answer is effected well before this point is reached. In precisely the same case is Ex. 127c, 127d, and 127h. (Compare bars three and seven of Ex. 127h.)

As we shall see, certain theorists have made the fundamental error of assuming that the rest in the 'head-and-tail' type invariably marks the point of *tonal* division in subject and answer alike.

As these examples were not sought out especially to illustrate this particular point, but merely noted as they came to hand, it may be confidently assumed that their pattern of tonal design is characteristic in general of the modulating subject that answers to the structures described in (ii) and (iii) of this chapter. The very fact that they all conform to a regular pattern strongly suggests their adherence to one unifying basic principle of design; and this, it would seem, is the same as that underlying the tonal design of binary form.

4.   *AFFINITY WITH BINARY FORM*

It would clearly be impossible to propose a tonal design as being typically representative of binary form, for the obvious reason that no two designs are necessarily the same. We are sometimes reminded that the first part of a binary movement concerns itself with the tonic and modulation to its 'sharp side', and the second part with modulation to its 'flat side'. Yet both the *Courante* and *Forlane* of Bach's first orchestral *Suite* in C touch upon the subdominant key at their outset; in the *Gigue* from his fifth *French Suite* on the other hand, the dominant key reappears towards the end of the second part. A further stumbling block in the way of such a plan would be the choice of key for ending the first part, for minor sometimes differ from major movements in this respect. But examination of such works as the keyboard suites of Bach and Handel suggests certain broad distinguishing features that are common to countless other binary movements.

(i) One such feature is that many binary movements end their first part with strongly established dominant tonality.

(ii) A second distinguishing feature common to many binary movements is a broad tonal design, wherein the first part is concerned mainly with tonic and dominant tonalities, and the second with modulation to nearly-related keys, which not infrequently includes the subdominant.

(iii) A third concerns the move *away* from the dominant key in the second part. In the majority of movements examined from Bach and Handel, it was found that the dominant key was seldom retained beyond a bar or two. In some movements, such as the *Gavotte, Polonaise*, and *Gigue* from the sixth *French Suite*, tonic tonality is restored in the very first bar of the second part by means of a contradictory accidental, so that the opening harmony of the second part is pivotal. (Dominant I = tonic V.) The relatively long stretch of dominant harmony in the second part of the *Courante* of Handel's fourteenth Clavier Suite was found to be rather exceptional.

(iv) A fourth distinguishing feature of the form is the occasional practice of reproducing the concluding bars of the first part at the corresponding place in the second part, suitably transposed to end the movement in the tonic key—a recapitulation in miniature, in fact. Examples of this are the *Gigues* of Bach's first and third *French Suites*, and the *Gigues* of Handel's seventh, eighth, and tenth Clavier Suites. In all these it amounts to nothing more than the reproduction of a few cadence bars; but in such movements as the *Air* in Bach's fourth *French Suite*, and the same composer's *Two-part Invention* No. 11 in F, it amounts to a near-complete recapitulation of the entire first part. A further feature common to both these movements is that their 'recapitulatory' sections set out in the subdominant key, in order finally to arrive back in the tonic. This subdominant-tonic move in the second part thus balances the tonic-dominant move of the first part.

(v) One final distinguishing feature of binary movements in general is the harmonic 'bridge' linking first and second parts, this being formed by commencing the second part with the same harmony as that concluding the first.

All the above features, incidentally, are contained in the *Air* from Bach's fourth *French Suite:*

(i) Its first part concludes in the dominant key of B flat.

(ii) Tonic tonality is restored in the very first bar of the second part by means of a contradictory A flat, dominant I thus becoming tonic V.

(iii) Its first part is concerned with tonic and dominant keys, and its second mainly with related keys, including the subdominant.

(iv) Its second part has a relatively long recapitulatory section.

(v) The two parts are bridged harmonically by the same chord.

Omitting for the present Ex. 126d and 126e, it will be seen that the remaining examples in Ex. 126 (pp. 120–6), and the whole of Ex. 127 (pp. 127–33), exhibit these same formal features. They all set out in the tonic, and end in the dominant. Subject and answer are bridged harmonically by the same chord. Their answers set out in the complementary key, and pass quickly back to tonic, where (apart from some possible incidental modulation) they remain. And just as Bach recalls briefly the dominant key in the second part of the

135

Gigue from his fifth *French Suite*, so this same tonality makes a fleeting reappearance in the answer in Ex. 127c.

Perhaps the most significant feature common to the modulating subject and binary form, is the abrupt move away from the dominant in the second part (answer) *irrespective of the proportionate balance of tonic and dominant keys in the first part (subject)*. Thus the three bars of dominant harmony in the first part of the *Air* are not reproduced proportionately in the opening bars of the second part. Compare this with what has been said in this connection concerning Exx. 126 and 127, and the affinity between subject and answer of fugal form and binary form becomes apparent.

Let us now see how Ex. 126d fits into the binary pattern. Seen as set out in Ex. 129, its close resemblance to the *Air*, and therefore to binary form, is unmistakable:

Ex. 129.   J. S. Bach, 'Forty-Eight', Book I, No. 18

Like the *Air*, the subject (first part) ends in the dominant. Dominant tonality in the answer (second part) is immediately contradicted by the E natural. Like the *Air*, subject and answer are bridged harmonically by the same chord. As in the *Air*, the return to the tonic key is made via the subdominant, so that the subject (first part) is concerned with tonic and dominant keys, which are balanced in the answer (second part) by subdominant and tonic.

The proportionate balance of tonic and dominant keys in the subject is not reproduced in the answer.

It thus contains in synthesis all the main distinguishing features of a binary movement. It remains of course, only an affinity, and nothing is claimed beyond that. It would be absurd, for example, to suggest that these binary principles were consciously applied; but at the same time, from the regular and consistently recurring pattern of formal and tonal design, it may not be unreasonable to ascribe these binary traits to a subconscious feeling for one of their 'everyday' forms.

5.   AN 'UNRECOGNIZED' TYPE OF MODULATING SUBJECT

There remains one other type to be considered, which although not singled out by textbooks as such, is nevertheless as much a modulating subject, involving similar questions of tonality and structure, as those already reviewed. Bach's chorale prelude, *Vom Himmel hoch da komm' ich her* illustrates the type admirably:

Ex. 130.   J. S. Bach, Chorale Prelude, Vom Himmel hoch da komm' ich her

It is not a modulating subject in the accepted textbook sense of the term (i.e. one that ends in the complementary key), but the harmonized entries in bars six and eleven show it modulating to dominant, and making a return modulation to tonic in its second bar. These moves (to dominant and back to tonic) are balanced by converse modulations at the corresponding points in the answer—hence its tonal form.[8]

It is important to appreciate that mutation must be effected at the answer's second note if modulation to the dominant key is to be staved off at this particular point.

This may be the opportune moment to stress that no particular significance should be attached to the scalic degrees of the notes involved in this particular mutation, i.e. seventh in subject, and third in answer. In Ex. 130 for example, a real reply to the subject's B (giving F sharp in the answer) must destroy the movement's consciously balanced tonal design—hence mutation being effected at this specific point. It will be appreciated therefore, that the actual point of mutation is decided solely by harmonic, and not melodic considerations. Criticized from this viewpoint the role of the note B in the process of mutation is seen as an effect, and not a cause. This is mentioned because certain theorists attach unwarranted significance to the leading note in instances of this kind, thereby muddling cause and effect. Their theories relating to this are discussed later in the chapter.

Let us now turn to the theorists' explanation of the modulating subject, viewed against this background.

6.   THE STANDARD TEXTBOOKS' APPROACH

Prout's explanation of modulating subjects, to which many subsequent writers are indebted, rests upon two main rules:

[8] Ex. 142a, 142b, 142c, and 142d on pp. 151–2 all answer to this same tonal design.

Rule I.[9] *'If the subject begin in the tonic, and modulate to the dominant, the answer must begin in the dominant and modulate to the tonic.'*[10]

Rule II. *'The modulation in the answer from dominant back to tonic must be made at the same point at which the modulation was made in the subject from tonic to dominant.'*[11]

These two main rules are supplemented by two subsidiary ones:

Rule III. 'A modulation should always be made as early as possible.'[12]

Rule IV. 'In a modulation from tonic to dominant consider the third and seventh of the tonic as sixth and third of dominant as soon as the modulation can be considered as having taken place, and answer them accordingly.'[13]

Each of these rules is now considered.

Rule I. As this constitutes normal procedure,[14] discussion is unnecessary. It is important to note, however, that Prout omits to mention the possibility of a return to the tonic via the key of the subdominant, as in Ex. 126d and 126e on pp. 122–3.

Rule II. Attention was drawn to this rule on pp. 133–4, where it was pointed out that although one may find examples exemplifying it, there are many others that prove it to be at variance with practice. Indeed, the 'tonic-triad' theory apart, it is doubtful whether there exists a wider breach between musical theory and practice, than that which separates Prout's rule from actual fact. Perhaps the label 'Prout's rule' is a little unfair to Prout, for subsequent writers' indebtedness to him (Gédalge, Macpherson, R. O. Morris, and Bairstow) is no less obvious than Prout's indebtedness to Higgs, who in turn, quotes the authority of Cherubini on this point. Gédalge for example, appears even more intent than Prout upon leaving no possible loophole for harmonic freedom:

Hence follow these two rules, which are applicable to all fugue subjects without exception:

Rule I. Every note, diatonic or chromatic which belongs in the subject to the scale of the key of the 1st. degree (principal key of the subject), must be reproduced in the answer by the note, diatonic or chromatic, found at the corresponding degree of the scale of the key of the 5th. degree of the subject, this fifth degree being taken as the tonic of the answer.

In this case, the answer imitates the subject *degree by degree*, or *accidental by accidental* [*altération par altération*] at the *fifth above* or the *fourth below*.

Rule II. Every note, diatonic or chromatic, which belongs in the subject to the scale of the key of the 5th. degree (this fifth degree becoming by modulation the tonic of the subject) must be reproduced in the answer by the note, diatonic or chromatic, found at the corresponding degree of the key of the 1st. degree of the subject (this first degree becoming the tonic of the answer while the subject keeps the fifth degree as tonic).

In this case, the answer imitates the subject *degree by degree*, or *accidental by accidental*, at the *fourth above* or the *fifth below*.[15]

The astonishing thing is, that with the overwhelming evidence of musical practice lined up against it, until recently this rule has been allowed to pass unchallenged. A. J. B. Hutchings must be one of the very few to challenge its validity: 'There is no authority in musical sense or in Bachian practice for the rule: "What has tonic harmony in S should have dominant harmony in A, and what has dominant harmony in S should have tonic harmony in A".'[16]

During the course of their research, these theorists must have come across many

---

[9] This numbering is arbitrary.
[10] *Fugue*, p. 49, para. 116.
[11] p. 50, para. 117.
[12] p. 67, para. 156.
[13] pp. 67–68, para. 156 (see also p. 53, para. 128, and p. 55, para. 131).
[14] Book I, No. 10 in E minor is an interesting exception. The apparent drift to the supertonic key of F sharp minor is abruptly arrested by a *Tierce de Picardie*.
[15] *Traité*, pp. 12–13, paras. 27–29.
[16] *Invention and Composition*, p. 91.

modulating subjects answering to a similar pattern as that in Exx. 126 on pp. 120–6 and 127 on pp. 127–33; that is, of the type in which the return modulation to tonic is made at the answer's outset, regardless of the point in the subject at which the converse modulation is effected; in other words, the type in which the point of modulation in subject and answer do not correspond, Rule II notwithstanding.

The purpose of Section 3 of this chapter (p. 133) is to endeavour to establish the point that tonally, subject and answer frequently move independently of one another. This, it was pointed out, is demonstrated in the score or so examples in Exx. 126 and 127. These same examples also demonstrate the unsoundness of Prout's rule. Yet regardless of the facts, Prout and others after him resorted to an ingenuous explanation that aimed at bringing all modulating subjects, their individual tonal designs regardless, within the rigid framework of Rule II. Applying his rule, Prout's line of reasoning for all modulating subjects alike, is that as the modulation *from* the dominant back to tonic is made at point X in the answer, then the modulation *to* the dominant must have been made at the corresponding point X in the subject. Only by reasoning thus could Rule II, which demands exact tonal balance between subject and answer, be justified. Let us see this theory applied to the subject and answer of Book I, No. 18 (Ex. 126d), which was fully discussed on p. 136.

Prout's contention is that the subject's first note only is in the tonic, and the remainder in the dominant: 'The following examples show the leading note very early in the subject treated as the third of the dominant, and answered by third of tonic. The following notes of the subject are all answered as belonging to the dominant key.'[17] (See Ex. 126d.)

Bairstow's explanation is similar: 'Occasionally, to avoid ugliness, it is necessary to regard the tonic as the subdominant of the dominant. . . .

'Similarly in the fugue in G sharp minor (Book I, No. 18) Bach preferred to regard the whole subject except the first note as being in D sharp minor, the second note to the seventh in the subdominant of that key, rather than alter the shape of bar 2. Thus, in the answer, this section is in C sharp minor, the subdominant of the tonic answering the subdominant of the dominant.'[18]

Gédalge takes the same view: 'Bach rightly considers it as modulating, starting from the second note to the key of the 5th degree.'[19]

Macpherson and A. W. Marchant[20] actually set it out as in Ex. 131. Macpherson's comment is, 'Here the Leading-note of G sharp minor is regarded as the *major* 3rd of the Dominant key, and answered by the *major* 3rd of the Tonic.'[21]

Ex. 131.   J. S. Bach, 'Forty-Eight', Book I, No. 18

These writers are merely repeating what Higgs had written of this same example many years earlier:

[17] *Fugue*, pp. 55–56, para. 132.
[18] *Counterpoint and Harmony*, p. 319.
[19] *Traité*, p. 35, para. 65.
[20] *Fugue Subjects*, p. 59, No. 337.
[21] *Counterpoint*, p. 106.

'[Ex. 131] shows the major third of the dominant (Fx) answered by the major third of the tonic (B♯), and the third of the tonic (B), really the sixth of the dominant, answered by the sixth of the tonic (E). This note rules the whole answer.'[22]

This roundabout method of explanation is arrived at by a reverse process of analysis, from answer back to subject, whereby the point of tonal division in the answer is related willy-nilly to the corresponding point in the subject. They all reason that as the move *from* the dominant key occurs at the second note of the answer, then to bring it into line with Rule II, it must follow that the move *to* the dominant key must occur at the second note of the subject. We thus see the process of reasoning whereby subjects and answers of this tonal design are adroitly manoeuvred by theoretical wrangling into complying with Rule II's condition, that 'The modulation in the answer from dominant back to tonic must be made at the same point at which the modulation was made in the subject from tonic to dominant.'

But it would be reasonable to claim, surely, that the subject of Book I, No. 18, is no more in the dominant key from its second note onwards, than is the answer in the tonic key from *its* second note onwards. The ear is the only guide, and nothing will convince the ear that the opening bar of the subject is in any key other than the tonic, any more than are the second to seventh notes of the answer in any key other than the subdominant. Their circuitous method of analysis arises from the fact that this example presents a case of a subject and answer involving three tonalities (tonic, dominant, and subdominant), which exceeds the limited tonal scope of Rule II. Concerned as it is with two tonalities only (tonic and dominant), this rule does not allow for the possibility of a return to the tonic key via the subdominant, hence their analysis of the answer's second note as 'the major third of the tonic', instead of, simply, the leading note of C sharp minor. It is probable that this method of analysis became established as a consequence of the following rule: 'this [a transient modulation to the subdominant] is always to be carefully avoided, as the only proper answer to the tonic is the dominant. . . . the rule that the answer should never be constructed in the key of the subdominant is a throughly sound one.'[23] There are sufficient musical examples in this chapter to demonstrate that the rule has no foundation in practice.

Another oft-quoted subject used to illustrate Rule II is Book I, No. 7, in E flat. Macpherson quotes it to illustrate his rule, which is virtually the same as Prout's: 'If a Subject modulates to the key of the Dominant, the Answer will make a return movement to the Tonic key at a corresponding point.'[24] He sets it out as in Ex. 132:

Ex. 132.   J. S. Bach, 'Forty-Eight', Book I, No. 7

Yet Ex. 128 on p. 134 shows the answer as being in the tonic key throughout. A second entry of the answer (bar ten) is again harmonized in the tonic key throughout. In common with Exx. 126 and 127 it is a further instance of what we might conveniently term *harmonic* mutation and *melodic* mutation being effected independently of each other. As in Exx. 126

---

[22] *Fugue*, p. 23.
[23] E. F. Richter, *Canon and Fugue*, p. 49.
[24] *Counterpoint*, p. 103.

and 127 the balance of tonality in subject and answer between tonic and dominant weighs heavily in favour of the former, thus badly upsetting Rule II.

This same example uncovers a further discrepancy between theory and practice. As will be demonstrated more fully later, theory makes the error of assuming that mutation automatically signifies modulation.

A final example (Ex. 133), which is quoted as set out in A. W. Marchant's *Fugue Subjects and Answers*,[25] shows the application of Rule II and the 'subdominant of the dominant' theory pushed to its furthest limits:

Ex. 133. SALA, FROM A. W. MARCHANT'S FUGUE SUBJECTS AND ANSWERS

In summarizing this discussion of Rule II, it becomes clear that these complicated explanations need never have arisen had it been recognized that mutation and the return modulation in the answer are frequently effected independently of each other; that mutation does not necessarily imply modulation, and that a third tonality (the subdominant) has at times to be reckoned with. From the many examples that have been given, it is equally clear that theory cannot hope to devise one single harmonic formula capable of embracing modulating subjects and answers in general.

Rule III. 'A modulation should always be made as early as possible.' This is supplemented by: 'The general practice of the great composers is *to regard the modulation as being made at the earliest possible point. . . .*'[26]

Prout appears to be the first theorist to have made these particular points, which have been reiterated successively by such writers as Macpherson and Bairstow. Modulation surely must depend upon spontaneous musical impulse, and it becomes difficult to reconcile the idea of a modulation as taking place at any point other than where it actually does. This may appear an all-too obvious statement of fact until we recall that Prout, Gédalge, Macpherson, and Bairstow all ask us to believe that although the subject of Book I, No. 18, is still in the tonic, Bach is thinking in terms of the dominant key from its second note onwards; that the composer is simultaneously writing in one key and thinking in terms of another.

Rule III became necessary in order to justify the curious anomalies that were bound to result from the restricted tonal formula of Rule II. Let us attempt to substantiate this contention.

The tonal design of the subject and answer from Sala (Ex. 133) is identical with that of Book I, No. 18:

Subject = Tonic—dominant;
Answer = Dominant—subdominant—tonic;

a design that finds no place in the restricted tonic-dominant formula of Rule II. Having forced Sala's subject and answer into the framework of Rule II, Marchant's analysis can be explained away only by the odd claim that the composer commences to think in terms

[25] *Fugue Subjects*, p. 32, No. 183.
[26] *Fugue*, p. 51, para. 121.

of the dominant key from the subject's second bar onwards (i.e. in the 'subdominant of the dominant'), even though it has not yet left the tonic. Hence the necessity for Rule III.

It is not surprising that Prout has ultimately to admit, 'Sometimes, however, the form of the subject does not admit of an early change.' After quoting the subject and answer of Ex. 127c he continues, 'It is impossible here to regard the modulation as taking place till after the subdominant harmony at (a). [i.e. the F natural in bar five].'[27]

Prout's explanation is upset by Bach's behaviour in the somewhat similar situation in his *Magnificat*, Ex. 126l on p. 126. As in Ex. 127c on p. 128, the subdominant (G) appears in bar two, which according to Prout's reasoning should preclude the possibility of mutation in the answer until the corresponding point had been left behind. But we see that far from being delayed until after this point, mutation is effected at the very outset of the answer's course. The free distribution of tonalities between subject and answer might well be examined against the background of Rule II. The exchange of a tone for a semitone between the ninth and tenth notes of the subject and answer automatically *precludes* the possibility of equally balanced tonalities. In order to justify itself in a case such as this, Rule II must analyse the *Magnificat* subject and answer as set out in Ex. 134; in turn, Rule III would justify this analysis by claiming that Bach commenced thinking of his subject as being in the key of the dominant (i.e. the subdominant of the dominant) from its second note onwards:

Ex. 134. J. S. BACH, MAGNIFICAT

It takes us back to our starting point; that although certain modulating subjects and answers do exhibit a just balance of tonalities between tonic and dominant keys (as in the group of Ex. 125 on pp. 114–17), there are just as many others that do not. As Rule II made no allowance for these exceptions it became necessary to promulgate a supplementary rule in order to bring these exceptions into line—hence Rule III.

The distribution of tonalities in the subject and answer of Ex. 126l on p. 126 is quite different from any other example of modulating subject and answer quoted, and thus serves to underline the whole point of the current chapter (and Hutchings's point also (p. 138)), that the tonal design of no two modulating subjects and their companion answers is necessarily alike.

It would appear therefore, that the role of the textbook should be that of directing a student's attention to the very freedoms in the matter rather than that of attempting to devise a set of rules which are bound to be doomed from the start.

Rule IV. 'In a modulation from tonic to dominant consider the third and seventh of the tonic as sixth and third of dominant as soon as the modulation can be considered as having taken place, and answer them accordingly.'[28]

In the Preface of his *Fugue*, Prout acknowledges his debt to Higgs's 'admirable Primer on *Fugue*'.[29] His debt to Higgs for Rule IV is plain. Higgs's rules are:

---

[27] p. 53, para. 126.
[28] The rules given by Gédalge are virtually the same (*Traité*, pp. 17–18, para. 38, and pp. 30–32, paras. 57–60).
[29] pp. iv-v.

'The answer is *tonal* when the subject modulates. Distinguish third of tonic from sixth of dominant; answer the former by third of dominant, and the latter by sixth of tonic.

'Distinguish the seventh used as a note of melodic embellishment from the seventh as third of dominant; answer the last by third of tonic.'[30]

Prout's Rule IV follows a detailed explanation of this 'double-relationship' theory, part of which is:

The next question is, when there is a modulation, at what point are we to consider it as taking place? The general practice of the great composers is *to regard the modulation as being made at the earliest possible point, and from that point to consider every note in its relation to the new key.*

That the student may quite clearly understand what is meant by this, we will take all the notes in the scale of C major, and show how each can be correctly answered in two ways, according to the point of view from which it is looked at. Supposing our fugue to be in the key of C, and that a modulation to the dominant occurs in the subject, the answer to each note will depend on whether that note comes before or after the modulation:—

C, if regarded as tonic of C, will be answered by G; but if regarded as the subdominant of G, it will be answered by F, the subdominant of C.[31]

There is no need to quote the rest of his paragraph, which continues in like fashion, through each of the scale's remaining degrees. Later, he adds, 'It is very important to be able to tell when answering a subject that modulates, in which of its two possible aspects any note is to be regarded. The only notes with which any difficulty is likely to be found are the third and the seventh of the tonic, which are also the sixth and third of the dominant. An examination of the fugues of the great masters will guide us in laying down definite rules for the treatment of both these notes.'[32]

The weakness of this system lies in its own basic error of assuming that mutation is determined solely by melodic considerations. In the discussion on *Structure* it was suggested that although mutation is apparent through the *melody*, the actual point at which it is effected is determined by *harmonic* considerations. This contention thus runs counter to the Higgs-Prout theory, which assumes *melody* to be the determining factor.

In opening the discussion on Rule IV, a first question that might be asked is—why should special significance be accorded the third and seventh degrees? If we consider for a moment the melodic construction of a number of fugue subjects that open on the tonic (the 'Forty-Eight' for example), it will become apparent that a subject's second note is far more likely to be the scale's upper second, third, fifth, or lower seventh, than either the upper fourth, or sixth degrees. In the 'Forty-Eight' (Book I, No. 5 excepted) none of the thirty subjects commencing on the tonic opens with a direct leap to either the upper fourth or sixth degrees.[33]

Ex. 134 (p. 142) from Bach's *Magnificat* in which the major second between the first two notes of the subject is exchanged for a repetition of the same note in the answer, demonstrates a potential source of embarrassment which could result from a mutation between the scale's first and second degrees. So that by a process of elimination (the leap from first to fifth degrees apart), we may conclude that a scale's first and third, and first and lower seventh degrees are likely to be involved in the process of mutation far more

---

[30] *Fugue*, p. 32. Richter had already devised similar formulae in the second edition of *Lehrbuch der Fuge*, and certain similarities of phrase suggest that Higgs's thinking here was guided by Richter's principles. (See E. F. Richter, *Canon and Fugue*, trans. F. Taylor, London, 1878, pp. 44–50, and compare with Higgs, *Fugue*, pp. 21–22, paras. 49–52.)

[31] *Fugue*, p. 51, paras. 121–2.

[32] p. 53, para. 127.

[33] See pp. 20 concerning subjects that open with a leap from the tonic to their lower fifth degree.

frequently than other degree relationships. Hence the prominence accorded the third and seventh degrees in the Higgs-Prout theory.

As a preliminary to the main discussion, consider first Ex. 135a, an 'indivisible' structural pattern:

Ex. 135A. Buxtehude, Organ Prelude and Fugue in C

According to the 'double-relationship' theory, Buxtehude regarded the third C of the subject as the subdominant of G, and answered it by F, the subdominant of C. Would it not be simpler, and at the same time more to the point, to say it is the harmony (the V–I cadence in C) that creates opportunity for mutation, out of which the melody evolves its altered form? Harmony and melody thus represent cause and effect respectively. Buxtehude might have answered the subject as in Ex. 135b:

Ex. 135B.

but by introducing the F natural at the right moment (becoming the seventh of V_2^4), it enables him to retain the conjunct line of the subject, and reproduce the same harmonic cell at the corresponding point in the answer. With the alternative of three C's in a row, this subject creates a situation that cannot possibly be solved by resort to Higgs's mathematical formula.

Next consider one of Prout's rules concerning the seventh degree: 'If a subject modulates, the leading note must be always treated as the third of the dominant, and answered by third of tonic...'[34] Ex. 125f and 125h on pp. 117–18 from Albrechtsberger, and Ex. 136 from Knecht are three instances in which this rule 'doesn't work'.

---

[34] *Fugue*, p. 55, para. 131.

Ex. 136. KNECHT, FUGUE IN D

Prout's comment on the E major example from Albrechtsberger (a surprising quotation in that it negates his own rule concerning the seventh degree) is, 'Our next example
shows . . . an octave in the subject becoming a seventh in the answer. . . . The first G is
treated as third of tonic, and the second as sixth of dominant.'[35]

The fact that the octave is exchanged for a seventh, and the two G's accorded different
treatment, is relatively unimportant; it is incidental, and Prout's comment merely draws
attention to the *consequences* of mutation, leaving the means whereby it is effected unex-
plained.

Again, would it not be simpler to say that it is the V–I cadence in B major (bars seven—
eight) that creates opportunity for mutation, of which the melody avails itself? Analyzed
from this viewpoint, the need for a mathematical formula does not arise; moreover, there
are no exceptions to the rule, simply because no rule is necessary.

These considerations apart, the real importance of these three examples is not in the
fact that they constitute exceptions to the rule relating to the tonic's seventh degree, but that
they serve to expose the rule's basic weakness, which is the wholly exaggerated importance
it accords, in modulating subjects of this type, to the role played by *melody*.

In all three cases, by 'treating the leading-note as third of dominant', mutation could
be effected equally well from each answer's second note,[36] but with this difference (and
herein lies the crux of the matter), that all three would now emerge with a quite different
tonal complexion. In place of the just balance of tonic and dominant tonalities between
subject and answer as at present, they all three would come into line with Ex. 126d (Book I,
No. 18), in that they would by-pass the dominant key, regaining the home tonic instead via
the key of the subdominant. It is by their *delaying* mutation beyond this point (i.e. the
answer's second note) that subdominant channels are avoided.

With both these mutation points open to them, each yielding a different tonal design
from the other, the composers' decision to opt for the course that they did suggests that
they attached at least equal importance to the ultimate harmonic outcome, as to the
answer's melodic shape.

We could pursue the matter further by conjecturing the reason behind these composers' decision to break the answer where they did. In Ex. 125f for example, it may not be
unreasonable to propose that Albrechtsberger, in avoiding subdominant tonality during
the exposition, was influenced by the fact of that key's use for a subsequent middle entry—
in other words, from consideration of the movement's *overall* tonal design.

In the more detailed discussion that now follows, Prout's theories concerning the
third and seventh degrees are discussed separately. First a summary of his rules and comments pertaining to the seventh degree:

[35] p. 59, para. 140.
[36] Compare the line of the subject of Ex. 125f on p. 117, for example, with that of Ex. 142c on p. 152.

(i) 'In a modulation from tonic to dominant consider the . . . seventh of the tonic as . . . third of dominant as soon as the modulation can be considered as having taken place, and answer [it] accordingly.'[37]

(ii) 'If a subject modulates, the leading note must be always treated as the third of the dominant, and answered by third of tonic . . .'[38]

(iii) 'So strongly is the leading note felt as the third of the dominant that it is not seldom answered by the third of the tonic, even when there is no modulation.'[39]

His supporting examples will be discussed later.

One of the most convincing arguments against his theory is, of course, the number of cases in which the seventh is *not* answered tonally—modulation or no modulation. They are far too numerous to be dismissed lightly as 'exceptions to the rule'. Three examples have just been given upsetting (ii). In turn (iii) is upset by Book I, No. 4, and Book II, Nos. 8 and 13. Further examples upsetting this are given in Ex. 137a–137c. To these many more could be added. These examples also raise the question of why a composer should 'feel strongly' the leading note as the third of the dominant on some occasions, and not on others.

Ex. 137A. J. S. Bach, Organ Fugue in D

Ex. 137B. J. S. Bach, Clavier Fugue in E minor (unfinished)

Ex. 137C. J. S. Bach, Cantata, Nun komm, der Heiden Heiland

A second major weakness of his theory concerns the character and function of the leading note. Is it likely that the leading note, the most powerful functionary of the Baroque's tonal system, would be 'felt' as anything other than what it was—the leading note?

[37] pp. 67–68, para. 156.
[38] p. 55, para. 131.
[39] p. 56, para. 133.

146

A third major weakness exposes itself in Prout's analysis of such examples as Ex. 126d and 126e on pp. 122–3. Of the former Prout writes:

'The following [example] show[s] the leading note very early in the subject treated as the third of the dominant, and answered by third of tonic';[40] and of the latter:

'[The] G sharp is considered not as the leading note of A minor, but as the chromatic major third of the dominant, and it is accordingly answered by the major third of the tonic.'[41]

The weakness lies in his analysis of the B sharp in Ex. 126d and the C sharp in Ex. 126e as the 'major third of the tonic', i.e. the tonic chromatic chord. Whether a combination such as this constitutes a true chromatic chord, or whether it is chord V in the subdominant key, is determined by the immediate context. According to Prout's own rule on the matter (quoted on p. 110) neither case can be regarded as a true tonic chromatic chord, as both their resolutions clearly prove them to be V in the key of the subdominant. The presence of the seventh of V in both examples weakens Prout's theory even further.

Mutation involving the seventh degree of the scale. Remembering that a real answer to the tonic's seventh degree automatically opens up dominant channels, it follows that mutation involving this degree is likely to be concerned with questions of tonal design. The two main reasons for mutation are:

(i)   To defer modulation to the dominant key. (This is not infrequently accomplished by the expedient of tonally answering the interval of a fifth by a fourth.)

(ii)   To maintain a just balance of tonic and dominant tonalities between subject and answer.

Discussion of (i).

Ex. 138.   Kuhnau, Clavier Suite in D

[40] pp. 55–56, para. 132.
[41] p. 52, para. 125.

Ex. 138 from Kuhnau, is an excellent illustration of a composer resorting to the expedient of mutation with the express object of *deferring* modulation. The extract is to the double bar of a binary movement fugal gigue; it is characteristic of the form that modulation to the dominant should appear rather towards the close of the first part than at its opening. A real answer at the opening of Ex. 138 inevitably must disturb this tonal balance, hence the composer's resort to mutation, by which means tonic tonality is retained, characteristically, through the greater part of the movement's first section. It will be noticed that the cross-answering of the tonic and dominant notes provides the means to this end. Most important of all, this example enables us to see the seventh degree in proper perspective; its role is a passive one, wholly an effect and not a cause. It would therefore be misplaced to claim that Kuhnau 'felt' the leading note as the third of the dominant.

Ex. 139a and 139b illustrates the same point:

Ex. 139A.   J. P. KRIEGER, KEYBOARD FUGUE IN C

Ex. 139B.   J. G. WALTHER, CHORALE PRELUDE, ACH GOTT UND HERR

The tonal reply to the tonic and dominant notes of the subject enables Krieger's little movement, apart from the slightly 'enhanced' dominant colouring, to remain firmly in the tonic key throughout. The tonal design of Ex. 139b, from J. G. Walther, in which modulation to the dominant is effectively delayed by the same means until well beyond the exposition, is a similar case. In both these examples, the role of the seventh degree is again a purely passive one.

Although this is not strictly relevant, it might be added that a tonally answered seventh degree is but one way of checking a move to the dominant. It is checked in Book I, No. 4 in C sharp minor by the unexpected, but beautifully introduced, 'flattened leading-note' (bar six), a device sometimes referred to as 'inganno'.[42] A more obvious device is seen in Ex. 140:

Ex. 140.   IBID.

This device (the answering of tone by semitone and *vice versa*) is discussed in Chapter VII.

Discussion of (ii). Mutation involving the seventh degree is frequently effected in order to achieve tonal balance. The principle involved has already been discussed (on pp. 136–7), and illustrated by the chorale prelude, *Vom Himmel hoch*. (Ex. 130.) It shows the tonic-dominant-tonic tonalities of the subject balanced by a converse order of tonalities in the answer. Here too, the just balance between these two tonalities is maintained by the expedient of replying tonally to the subject's B natural. I write 'B natural' and not 'seventh degree' deliberately, because this same example exposes the unsoundness of Higgs's theory in yet another direction; for as Bach consistently effects a modulation to the dominant between the subject's first and second notes, it follows that the B is no longer the seventh degree of the tonic, but the third degree of the dominant *key*. This example thus calls in question a rule that exhorts us to regard the seventh as third of the dominant, when it already *is* the third of the dominant, and as such possesses none of the leading note's characteristics.

Ex. 135a on p. 144 from Buxtehude provides a further example of this. The B in the subject (harmonized as the third of the dominant *key*) becomes E in the answer, the third of a firmly restored tonic key.

Ex. 141 is a complex study of tonal interplay between subject and answer:

Ex. 141.   BUXTEHUDE, ORGAN PRELUDE AND FUGUE IN F

---

[42] See also his F major Organ Prelude (Toccata) and Fugue (BWV 540), bar ten.

The subject's initial dominant, reiterated over its opening three bars, is first replied to tonally by the answer's F over *its* opening three bars. Melodic adjustment in the answer is then effected to normal dominant level at (a) in bar nine. The subject's V-I tonic key cadence at (b) in bar four, is balanced by a parallel V-I dominant key cadence in the answer at (c) in bar ten. Conversely, the subject's implied V-I dominant key cadence at (d) in bars five and six, is balanced by a parallel V-I tonic key cadence in the answer at (e) in bars eleven and twelve. This balance is made possible only by resorting to a second mutation in the answer at (f) in bar ten. Thus the subject's modulation from F major to its dominant, is balanced by the answer's modulation from B flat major to *its* dominant. (Had mutation not been resorted to at (f), the cadence at (e) would have been formed in G major, which lies outside the related key circle.) A third and final mutation at (g) in bar twelve enables the answer to finish in the dominant.

Viewed in perspective against the complex tonal design of the whole, the mutation involving the seventh degree (compare the E in bar four with the A in bar ten) appears relatively insignificant, in that it merely provides the means to the end.

A few supporting examples are added:

Ex. 142A.　J. S. Bach, Prelude Fugue and Allegro for Lute or Clavier

Ex. 142B.　J. G. Walther, Preludio con Fuga

Ex. 142c. C. P. E. Bach, Fugue in A

Ex. 142d. Schwenke, Organ Fugue in C

Ex. 142e. Pachelbel, Chorale Prelude, Vom Himmel hoch, da komm ich her

Ex. 142F. BUXTEHUDE, ORGAN PRELUDE AND FUGUE IN E

S. (2nd entry)

A.

Ex. 142G. KIRNBERGER, CHORAL FUGUE IN B FLAT

All seven have this same feature—the modulation to the dominant in the subject is balanced by tonic tonality at the corresponding place in the answer. In some cases the result is an almost complete reversal of the more usual tonal balance between subject and answer; such a case is Ex. 142g, where the subject (apart from its initial note) is in the key of the *dominant;* and the answer (apart from *its* initial note) in the key of the *tonic*.

Clearly then, the reason for mutation involving the so-called seventh degree in all cases quoted (and to these may be added Ex. 126f, p. 123) is restoration of tonic tonality.

The prominently placed tonic and dominant notes in the subjects of Exx. 130 (p. 137), and 142a–142g could possibly be considered a further, but certainly not the main, cause of their tonal answers. (Pachelbel's setting of *Vom Himmel hoch, da komm ich her* (Ex. 142e), might usefully be compared with Bach's setting of the same tune in Ex. 130.)

It remains to examine a few examples quoted by various theorists. First, Prout's comment on Book I, No. 19 in A major: 'So strongly is the leading note felt as the third of the dominant that it is not seldom answered by the third of the tonic, even when there is no modulation.'[43] This is no different from Higgs's comment on the same example: 'The second note of the subject is rather felt as third of the dominant than as seventh of the scale, and is accordingly answered by the third of the tonic.'[44]

Accessibility of the 'Forty-Eight' renders quotation unnecessary, but reference to the score will show the tonal design of the exposition as being similar to the group just examined, in that the tonality of subject and answer alike is part-tonic and part-dominant. It thus proves Prout incorrect in his observation, 'even when there is no modulation'. The tonal reply is necessary in order to achieve this tonal balance.

A. W. Marchant falls into the same error in his analysis of Ex. 143 from Mozart's *Requiem* (K.626) when he writes, 'The C sharp at * in subject is here considered as 3rd of dom., as it is answered by F sharp the 3rd of tonic, although there is no real modulation to the dom., and it is rather felt to be leading note of tonic'[45]—for the alto entry of the subject shows that there is modulation to the dominant, which is balanced by tonic harmony at the corresponding place in the answer.

Ex. 143.   MOZART, REQUIEM, K.626

[43] *Fugue*, p. 56, para. 133.
[44] *Fugue*, p. 23.
[45] *Fugue Subjects*, p. 90, No. 482.

An oft-quoted subject in this same connection is Book I, No. 23 in B major:

Ex. 144.   J. S. BACH, 'FORTY-EIGHT', BOOK I, No. 23

A. W. Marchant comments, 'This example [Ex. 144] shows the 7th of the scale (A ♯) in its two relations:- first, at * as 3rd of dom., answered by D♯ 3rd of tonic; second, at ⊕ as leading note of tonic, answered by E♯, leading note of dom.'[46]   Macpherson follows Prout's line of reasoning: 'Most of the greatest fugal writers, notably J. S. Bach himself, often prefer to think of the Leading-note . . . as the 3rd of the Dominant key, rather than as the 7th of the Tonic key. . . .   So markedly does Bach manifest this preference, that he sometimes treats the Leading-note in this way, even when the S. does *not* actually modulate to the Dominant key.'[47] Bairstow's analysis is similar: '[Ex. 144] would normally be regarded as being entirely in B, and would have a real answer . . . Bach took the unusual view that the notes under the square bracket [i.e. second to fifth notes of S] were in F sharp and thus arrived at the tonal answer.'[48]

[46] p. 66, No. 371.
[47] *Counterpoint*, pp. 105–6.
[48] *Counterpoint and Harmony*, p. 318.

As in his analysis of Ex. 126d (Book I, No. 18), Bairstow again asks us to accept that Bach simultaneously is writing in one key and thinking in another. In any case, the unsoundness of Bairstow's contention is made apparent by the fact that all four entries of the subject of Book I, No. 23 (bars five, eleven, twenty-one, and twenty-nine) are harmonized in the tonic key throughout. A more likely explanation surely, is that Bach is replying tonally to the subject's first and fifth notes, i.e. tonic and dominant,[49] and that the melodic contour of the subject (the interposition of supertonic between tonic and dominant) necessarily involves a two-fold mutation in the answer. (See pp. 38–43.) That leading note is not replied to by leading note is merely a consequence of this. One result of this tonal answer is that tonic tonality is retained part-way through the answer's course in both exposition entries, and in its final entry in bar thirty-one. It thus assumes quite a different character from the wholly dominant entry in bar sixteen.

Bairstow's analysis shows him falling into the error (to which passing reference was made on p. 141) of assuming that mutation automatically implies modulation. Exx. 138 (p. 147–8), 139a, and 139b (p. 148) prove that it does not. Indeed, far from implying modulation, these three examples, together with Book I, No. 23, show that mutation is sometimes resorted to in order to *counter* a modulation. Bairstow is not alone in this. The same inference must be drawn from Prout's curious censure of Mozart: 'Sometimes a composer has chosen to consider a modulation implied where there is no real necessity for it.'

Ex. 145.   MOZART, QUARTET IN D MINOR, K.173

'Here a real answer . . . would have been much more usual, and (with all respect to Mozart, be it said) much better. The threefold repetition of D spoils the form of the answer.'[50]

Paradoxically, some half-century earlier, we see Cherubini condemning in his own work, the very form of answer (a real one) that Prout would substitute for Mozart's tonal one: 'The subject of this fugue belongs to tonal fugue, as it descends first from the tonic to the dominant; therefore, the response should go from the dominant to the tonic.'

Ex. 146.   CHERUBINI, FUGUE IN D MINOR

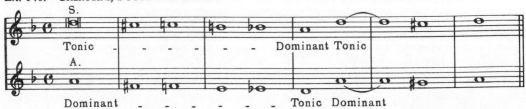

'But this response would have rendered the working of the counter-subjects extremely difficult, and would have compelled frequent changes. It has been judged fit, therefore, to treat it as a real fugue.'[51]

---

[49] It is interesting to compare Book I, No. 23 with Ex. 142a on p. 151. It will be seen that the melodic sequence of the first eight notes of S. and A. alike is identical.

[50] *Fugue*, p. 64, para. 150.

[51] *Counterpoint and Fugue*, p. 90.

This, incidentally, provides the clue to Mozart's reply, which is nothing more than a tonal response to the subject's tonic and dominant. And Mozart's answer is backed by the earlier authority of Fux:

Ex. 147. Fux, from A. W. Marchant's Fugue Subjects and Answers

An example from Eberlin illustrates the same point:

Ex. 148. Eberlin, Organ Toccata and Fugue in D

This example is in need of little comment beyond pointing out that mutation (involving the seventh degree) is resorted to in order to reply tonally to the subject's tonic and dominant.

A further case in point is Prout's analysis of the subject and answer from Mozart's C major Mass:

Ex. 149A. Mozart, Mass in C, K.258

Prout comments: 'This is a curious example, because Mozart by the way he answers the subject implies three modulations—to the dominant and back in bar 2, and again to the dominant at the end. It would have been simpler to treat the first F sharp, which is almost immediately contradicted, as a chromatic note, and to have given the answer the following form—'

Ex. 149B.

'which would have been equally correct here.'[52]

Prout misses the whole point of Mozart's answer (quoted in full in Ex. 149c), which is a tonal reply to the subject's tonic and dominant:

Ex. 149C.   MOZART, MASS IN C, K.258

This enables the dominant *tonality* at the beginning and ending of the subject to be balanced by tonic *tonality* at the corresponding places in the answer which, incidentally, remains in the tonic key throughout. Prout's alternative answer upsets this tonal balance completely.

A final example in this group is set out in Ex. 150 as quoted by A. W. Marchant.[53] It shows his falling into the same error, for this short twelve-bar fugue concerns itself with tonic and subdominant tonalities only.[54]

Ex. 150.   GOTTLEIB MUFFAT, CLAVIER TOCCATA AND FUGUE IN A

[52] *Fugue*, p. 60, para. 142.
[53] *Fugue Subjects*, p. 65, No. 367.
[54] See *Denkmäler der Tonkunst in Österreich*, Graz, 1960, Vol. 58, p. 29.

Mutation involving the third degree of the scale. Prout's rule is, 'As we have to regard every note in its relation to the new key as early as possible, the third should be considered as the sixth of the dominant, and answered by the sixth of the tonic . . . excepting, 1st, when it comes between other notes of the tonic chord, or is followed immediately by the tonic; and 2nd, when the subsequent appearance of the subdominant in the subject shows that the modulation cannot yet have taken place.'[55]

As with the seventh degree, the significance attached to the third degree is wholly unwarranted. Much of what has been said concerning the seventh degree applies equally here. It is merely consequential for example, if during the course of an answer to a modulating subject, the third emerges as 'the sixth of the dominant'. Like the seventh, its role in such cases is purely a passive one. This being so, further preliminaries are hardly necessary, and it remains only to examine and discuss examples.

Consider Ex. 151 from Buxtehude:

Ex. 151.   BUXTEHUDE, ORGAN PRELUDE AND FUGUE IN E

This is in no different case from Ex. 148 (p. 157), in that the tonal reply is given in order to cross-answer the subject's tonic and dominant. The fact that the scale's third degree (G sharp) emerges as the sixth degree (C sharp) in the answer, is merely a consequence of this. Its effect is that dominant tonality is staved off until the very end of the exposition.

Ex. 152 from Purcell is a further example, and provides us with a working basis:

Ex. 152.   PURCELL, TWELVE SONATAS OF THREE PARTS NO. 1

In its light let us consider Ex. 153a to 153d:

Ex. 153A.   ALBRECHTSBERGER, FUGUE IN C

Prout comments, 'This passage illustrates the partiality of fugue writers for treating the third of the tonic as the sixth of the dominant, and the leading note as the third of the dominant. There is no *necessity* for a tonal change till (a), and the answer might have been [as in Ex. 153b].'

Ex. 153B.

[55] *Fugue*, p. 53, para. 128.

'Here we have another example of what we have already seen more than once, that it is sometimes possible for a subject to have two different answers, both correct. The student will learn by experience, in such cases, which is the better.'[56]

The true explanation surely of the two-fold mutation in Albrechtsberger's answer, is that the first is made to allow for a tonal reply to the subject's tonic and dominant (first and ninth notes), and the second to restore tonic tonality. Prout's alternative answer in Ex. 153b eliminates the tonal answer. The tonal balance between this particular subject and answer might also be observed.

Ex. 153C. J. S. BACH, EIGHT LITTLE PRELUDES AND FUGUES, No. 1 IN C

Prout's comment on Ex. 153c is the same as he made about Ex. 145 from Mozart (see p. 156): 'Sometimes the great composers choose to consider a modulation as implied when there is no absolute necessity for it. Here [Ex. 153c] we see from the answer given by Bach that he implies a modulation in the second bar, though a real answer would have been perfectly correct. Had he regarded E as the third of C, he would have answered it by B, the third of G; but he regards it as the sixth of G, and therefore answers it by A, the sixth of C.'[57]

[56] pp. 60–61, para. 143.
[57] pp. 50–51, para. 120.

Prout's odd analysis is arrived at through the same erroneous assumption that mutation in the answer automatically implies modulation. Paradoxically, he is both right and wrong; right, because in this instance mutation *does* imply modulation, and wrong, because he is mistaken in saying that the subject does not modulate; for though not apparent through the melody, the full text shows that it does incorporate intermediate modulation, and that the tonal response is given in order to preserve a balance between tonic and dominant tonalities. The cadence in the dominant key at (a) in the subject, is balanced by a parallel cadence in the tonic key at (b) in the answer; and the move in the subject from tonic to dominant in bars seven and eight is balanced in the answer by a parallel move from the subdominant to *its* dominant in bars eight and nine. A further appearance of the subject in bar sixteen is similarly harmonized. A further point is that a strict answer to the subject's *harmonies* must involve the key of the supertonic (D major), a key not frequently found in the exposition.[58]

Although not actually expressed in the subject itself, this is one of many examples quoted of a subject modulating to dominant, and making a return modulation to tonic. More could be added to show that this particular tonal design is frequently to be found in Baroque practice. Prout's analysis of Ex. 153c would suggest that he failed to take this possibility into account. This suggestion is strengthened by a comment he makes in his chapter on the *Subject:* 'It is also possible, though somewhat rare, for a subject to begin in the tonic, modulate to the dominant and return to the tonic'.[59]

Ex. 153D. J. S. Bach, Cantata, Lobe den Herrn, den mächtigen König

[58] Prout himself makes this point: 'it must be added that we occasionally (we might also say exceptionally) find the dominant key answered by the supertonic, instead of by the tonic. Sometimes this is in an incidental modulation . . . Here the answer [Handel, *Dettingen Anthem*] is, to say the least of it, unusual.' (p. 62, para. 146.)

[59] p. 11, para. 37. Even his analysis of his supporting example (see Ex. 154*, p. 162) is rather odd—'If a subject begins in the tonic, modulates to dominant, and returns to tonic, the answer makes the converse modulations—from dominant to tonic, and back to dominant' [60]—for where in the answer are the two converse modulations he describes?

[60] p. 58, para. 138.

Prout comments: 'The following passage [Ex. 153d] shows the third in both aspects. The F's in the second bar of the subject prevent our regarding it as in the key of G; but at (a) the change is made at the earliest opportunity. The first E, being the resolution of the F in the preceding bar (the chord being the dominant seventh), must of course be the third of the tonic, and must be answered by B; the second E is treated as the submediant of G, and answered by the submediant of C—viz., A.'[61]

Structurally, this example belongs to what was termed the 'divisible type'. Mutation is effected in the answer following a V-I cadence in the dominant, which parallels a V-I tonic cadence at the corresponding point in the subject. These, surely, are the true means whereby a tonal reply is rendered possible.

Other examples quoted by Prout (in which the 'third is considered as the sixth of the dominant') have already been analyzed; they include Exx. 125a (pp. 114–15), 126b (p. 121), and 126g (p. 124). Further discussion would serve no real purpose. We pass on to discuss Ex. 155a from Handel's Concerto Grosso in C.

Ex. 155A.   HANDEL, CONCERTO GROSSO, ALEXANDER'S FEAST

*Ex. 154.   J. S. Bach, Cantata, Sehet, welch' eine Liebe.

[61] pp. 53–4, para. 128.

'In our next example' writes Prout, 'the change is not made at the earliest possible moment (in the first bar), for this would have disfigured the subject too much.

Ex. 155B.

'The mental effect of the music is distinctly that of the key of C, till we come to (a) where the double significance of the third of the scale is very clearly shown. The first E, being followed by C, is the third of the tonic, and is answered by the third of the dominant; the second E is not followed by a note of the tonic chord, and is therefore regarded as sixth of the dominant.'[62]

Here then, we find Prout compelled to admit to a further case in which his rule does not work out. While it is true that a tonal change following the first E would disfigure the subject, I would suggest that this in itself is not the real reason for Handel's avoiding mutation at this point. Even supposing mutation had not disfigured the subject at this point, we may be quite certain that Handel would still have effected mutation where he did, i.e. immediately following the V-I cadence in the dominant. (Subject and answer are given in full context in Ex. 125d on p. 116.) The technique here is precisely the same as that in Ex. 153d on p. 161.

The limitations of this theory expose themselves perhaps nowhere more fully than in Prout's analysis of Ex. 156a. He comments: 'The answering of one note by two is sometimes to be met with in the case of the dominant and supertonic, as in the following passage—'

Ex. 156A.   J. S. BACH, CLAVIER FUGUE IN A

'Here the supertonic at (a) is first answered by the supertonic of E, and then treated as dominant of E, and answered by dominant of A. Evidently had it been so regarded the first time, it would have utterly spoilt the answer.'[63]

Ex. 156B.

The text in full (Ex. 156c) shows that the answer at the point of mutation (see bar nine) is not in the key of A at all, but in the key of the subdominant, D:

Ex. 156C.   IBID.

[62] pp. 54–55, para. 130.
[63] p. 57, para. 136.

As in Book I, No. 18, a return to the tonic is made via the subdominant. The straight-forward explanation is that the answer derives its modified shape from the cadential harmonies.

From Prout's observations both here and elsewhere, it would appear that he was content to look no further than the initial appearance of subject and answer which became the foundation stone of his and others' method of analysis. This assumption is strengthened by the fact that incidental modulation of the type incorporated in *Vom Himmel hoch, da komm' ich her* (See Ex. 130, p. 137) and the C major Organ Fugue (Ex. 153c, p. 160) appears to have escaped his attention altogether.

CHAPTER VII

INTERVAL RELATIONSHIPS BETWEEN SUBJECT AND ANSWER

1. *CASES OTHER THAN SUSPENSIONS*

In the opening chapter, attention was drawn to Marpurg's rule concerning the strict preservation of the interval sequence between subject and answer (p. 13). Marpurg later reiterates this rule, during the course of an analysis of the subject and answer of Book I, No. 1, and concludes: 'The tonic c is answered by the dominant g, and all subsequent intervals are imitated with strict regard for the position of tones and semitones right to the very last note.'[1]

Both Prout and Kitson betray uneasiness concerning Bach's alleged freedoms in this respect, to the point that Prout prefers to align himself with Marpurg's rule, the contrary evidence of practice notwithstanding:

Though, as a general rule, the transposition of the subject a perfect fourth or fifth should be strictly carried out, we often find the position of the semitones disregarded, a semitone being answered by a tone, and a tone by a semitone. This is especially the case with the subdominant and leading note, as will be seen by the following passages . . .

Ex. 157A.   J. S. BACH, FUGHETTA ON ALLEIN GOTT IN DER HÖH' SEI EHR'

Ex. 157B.   J. S. BACH, MASS IN B MINOR

[1] *Abhandlung*, Part I, Chap. III, p. 24, Section I.

Ex. 157c. Mozart, Litany in B flat, K.125

On the same principle—the disregard of semitones—must be explained the occasional answering of a major by a minor third, or a minor by a major, in the course of a subject. . . .

Ex. 158a. J. S. Bach, Eight Little Preludes and Fugues, No. 8 in B flat

Ex. 158b. Handel, Muzio Scevola

Students are advised not to imitate such freedoms as these, but in all cases to preserve the position of the semitones, except, of course, at the moment of modulation.[2]

Kitson carries this a step further, by imposing alternative suggestions of his own:

A correct answer is always at the interval of a perfect fifth or fourth from the Subject. But Bach sometimes uses the diatonic lower auxiliary note, thus causing a divergence from the principle in unessentials: [Here Kitson quotes the subject and answer of Book II, Nos. 11 in F, and 1 in C.]

And cases could be quoted in which there seems to be no valid reason for the breach of the principle. Prout quotes the following case among others: [See Ex. 157a]. It is difficult to see why the Answer should not have been given thus:

[2] *Fugue*, pp. 61–62, paras. 144–5.

Ex. 159A.

Again, the same author quotes the following: [See Ex. 157b]. But there would not seem to be any objection to the answer given below [Ex. 159b]:[3]

Ex. 159B.

Kitson's opening sentence provides the clue to both his and Prout's misunderstanding of the principle involved, which accounts for their misplaced criticism of Bach's behaviour. As pointed out in an earlier chapter, the rule that the answer must be an exact reproduction of the subject in the key of the dominant, has no foundation in either Renaissance or Baroque practice. Fux was strict in the matter of correspondence in subject and answer of tones and semitones: 'A fugue, then, arises when a succession of notes in one part is repeated in another part, with due regard for the mode, and especially for the position of whole- and half-tone steps.'[4] But turning once again to his model, Palestrina, we find that examples are not wanting in which the sequence of tones and semitones between subject and answer is not strictly followed. One example has already been cited (Ex. 103, p. 98) and others are given in Ex. 160a and 160b:

Ex. 160A.   PALESTRINA, MASS, AD FUGAM

[3] *Fugal Construction*, pp. 23–25.
[4] *Gradus, The Musical Quarterly*, XXXVI (1950), p. 529.

Ex. 160B. IBID.

Had Palestrina here preserved a strict sequence, by the use of chromatic inflexion, the character of the mode would have been weakened;[5] by not doing so he keeps it undisturbed.

As in the case of mutation involving the scale's third and seventh degrees, the answering of a tone by a semitone, or a major by a minor third, or *vice versa*, is of no importance in itself, since its purpose and function is to control the course of the tonality.

A case in point is Ex. 42a on p. 41 from Purcell, which has already been quoted in this connection. (See p. 41.)

A further instance is the tenth variation of Bach's *Goldberg Variations*:

Ex. 161. J. S. BACH, GOLDBERG VARIATIONS, No. 10

[5] Thus distinguishing between Fugue and Imitation, of which earlier Fux writes: 'Imitation arises when one part follows another, after a number of rests, forming the same intervals with which the first part began and without any regard for the . . . position of whole- and half-tone steps.' (p. 527.)

Ex. 138 showed Kuhnau deliberately deferring modulation to the dominant in order to achieve tonal balance in a binary movement. (See pp. 147–8.)

Variation 10 (*Fughetta*) of the *Goldberg Variations* is a binary form movement, and here too, a real answer must inevitably guide the tonality into dominant channels. Whereas Kuhnau avoided this by the expedient of cross-answering tonic and dominant, Bach avoids it here by answering semitone by tone, and minor by major third, and *vice versa*. (Compare bars one and two with five and six.) Yet another adjustment in which a second in the subject is exchanged for a third in the answer, provides the means of further delaying the dominant key. (Compare bars two–three (**) with six–seven, and trace the effect of this on bar eight.) In consequence, dominant tonality is staved off successively until near the double-bar of the first part, resulting in the more usual tonal design of a binary form movement.

In Ex. 162, we see Brahms effecting a return modulation to the home tonic by precisely the same means:

Ex. 162.   BRAHMS, EIN DEUTSCHES REQUIEM

This example contains two further points of interest; first, it further upsets the textbook rule relating to the answering of the leading note by 'third of tonic'; and second, the tonic key in the answer is re-established well in advance of the melodic adjustment, which again runs counter to textbook ruling.

Tonal economy. The full context of *Allein Gott in der Höh' sei Ehr'* (Ex. 163) provides the answer to Kitson's query, 'It is difficult to see why the answer should not have been given thus' (as in Ex. 159a on p. 167), and also demonstrates why his alternative answer is unacceptable. He fails to see, apparently, that by answering all but the first and last notes tonally (at subdominant level), the tonic and dominant notes of the subject are conversely replied to by dominant and tonic. By this expedient, tonic tonality is retained throughout the entire exposition, and to a point well beyond it. It is a fine example of tonal economy:

Ex. 163.   J. S. Bach, Fughetta on Allein Gott in der Höh' sei Ehr'·

A further example of tonal economy is seen in Bach's C major Clavier Fugue (Ex. 164), where apart from a transient subdominant colouring, tonic tonality is again retained throughout the exposition:

Ex. 164.   J. S. Bach, Clavier Fugue in C

Quite clearly, this is rendered possible only by a diatonic response to the B of the subject. Comparison with Palestrina's *Mentre ch'al mar* (Ex. 103, p. 98) leaves its ancestry in little doubt. By resorting to this same device, Purcell is able to maintain tonic tonality well beyond the exposition in his Sonata No. 11 of *Sonatas of Three Parts*:

Ex. 165. PURCELL, TWELVE SONATAS OF THREE PARTS, NO. 11

Our final example illustrating tonal economy shows the initial drop of a seventh answered by a sixth, followed by a reversal of the original order of tones and semitones:

Ex. 166. BEETHOVEN, FUGUE IN C

Concerning this answer, Cockshoot writes:

The Answer begins reasonably enough, with tonic harmony balanced by dominant harmony, but at $4^{1/2}$ Beethoven answers the seventh with a sixth and writes G instead of F sharp. What could and should have continued as a real Answer ending on B at 5^1 becomes a patently incorrect one, which no appeal to the practice of the great masters can justify. Beethoven knew the correct form, and the incomplete entry at 8^3 continues far enough to show this. Had he written a correct real Answer, the Subject could not have entered at 5^1, and a codetta would have been necessary. It is impossible to believe that Beethoven baulked at the effort of contriving a codetta. More probable is it that he wanted his march-like Subject to appear at regular intervals of two bars, even if a little brutality had to be shown to the latter half of the Answer.[6]

I suggest that Beethoven's allegedly 'patently incorrect' answer *can* be justified, by appeal to the exposition of Bach's C major Clavier Fugue (Ex. 164, p. 170). It will be seen that the tonal design of the two expositions is identical, for apart from a transient sub-dominant colouring (in Beethoven's case a necessary resort to 'musica ficta'), they both retain tonic tonality throughout. Whereas Bach studiously staves off modulation to the dominant by the expedient of answering semitone by tone, Beethoven staves it off no less studiously by the devices outlined by Cockshoot himself. In both cases, the exposition is followed by a move to the key of the dominant. Beethoven thus uses slightly, but only slightly, different means to gain the same end.

A final point. If, as Cockshoot claims, 'Beethoven knew the correct form, and the incomplete entry at 8^3 continues far enough to show this', it is logical to presume, surely, that he must have had very good reason for using the 'incorrect' form.

Tonal balance. This same expedient is sometimes used as a means of maintaining tonic tonality part-way through the answer, as in Book II Nos. 11 and 21, and Ex. 167 from Handel:

Ex. 167.   HANDEL, MUZIO SCEVOLA

[6] J. V. Cockshoot, *The Fugue in Beethoven's Piano Music*, London, 1959, p. 31.

The text makes it clear that had Handel wished, by modifying slightly the accompanying counterpoint in the seventh bar (writing the last two quavers as B natural, C sharp),[7] the answer could have set out straightway in the dominant key. But from the answer he actually gives, it is equally clear that Handel did not want it that way; and it is by this same device that he re-establishes tonic tonality for the subject's second entry in bar fourteen. (Compare the interval sequence in bar six with bar twelve.) And if we glance back to Ex. 119 on p. 107, we see Handel replying to his subject at subdominant level of *pitch*, while adroitly manoeuvring the tonality into tonic and dominant channels, thus gaining the best of both worlds. The inevitable consequence is a quite different sequence of interval relationships between subject and answer. It is an extreme case, as there are no fewer than twelve deviations from the original sequence.

This device is, in fact, no more than another form of tonal answer, and is used here by Handel to precisely the same end as Bach used it in the group of tonally answered subjects from the 'Forty-Eight' (listed on p. 45), the common end being retention of tonic tonality part-way through the answer.

A less apparent form of tonal balance (or perhaps we should say tonal 'design') resulting from this same device, may be seen in two different types of modulating subjects: (i) those ending in a new key, and (ii) those ending in the same key, but incorporating incidental modulation.

Examples illustrating (i) come from Bach's B minor Mass (Ex. 168) and Mozart's Litany (Ex. 169).

Ex. 168.   J. S. BACH, MASS IN B MINOR

---

[7] cf *The Art of Fugue*, Contrapunctus XVI, bar eight of Inversus.

Ex. 169.   Mozart, Litany in B flat, K.125

The subject from the Mass is accompanied throughout. This shows it setting out in the dominant key, and ending in the tonic, and the answer[8] replying with converse modulation. By effecting mutation in the answer at the point he does, and by freely exchanging the quality of certain of its intervals, Bach achieves the following tonal designs:

Subject		Answer	
Dominant Key	*Tonic Key*	*Tonic Key*	*Dominant Key*
1½ bars	3½ bars	3½ bars	1½ bars

Kitson's alternative (Ex. 159b) is an unmodified transposition of the subject from its third bar onwards, which results in a completely different tonal complexion:

Subject		Answer	
Dominant Key	*Tonic Key*	*Tonic Key*	*Dominant Key*
1½ bars	3½ bars	1½ bars	3½ bars

He would thus gain his point of melodic symmetry at the cost of Bach's original tonal design. Mozart achieves the same end in Ex. 169, by resorting to this device. He makes a return modulation to the tonic key of B flat by means of a pivot harmony in bar fourteen. (I in F = V^7 in B flat.) A consequence of this is that the scalic run over chord V in bar six of the subject now takes place over chord I in the corresponding bar of the answer. (Bar fifteen.) Inevitably, the relative position of certain tones and semitones must become reversed. When viewed in perspective against the overall formal design, the matter of interval relationship appears quite insignificant.

The first example illustrating (ii) comes from Bach's B flat Organ Fugue, No. 8 of *Eight Little Preludes and Fugues*:

Ex. 170.   J. S. Bach, Eight Little Preludes and Fugues, No. 8 in B flat

---

[8] This could be regarded not as a subdominant answer, but as a further instance of a section setting out with the *answer*, which is replied to by the subject. This view gains strength from the fact that the alto entry in bar six is answered tonally by the soprano in bar thirteen.

This example has the same tonal design as *Vom Himmel hoch* (Ex. 130, p. 137) and the group in Ex. 142 (pp. 151–3), for although not apparent through the melody, the full text shows a modulation to the dominant between the first and second bars of the subject. (See bars thirteen and fourteen.) The dominant colouring in the subject is balanced by tonic tonality at the corresponding place in the answer at its first appearance in bars seven and eight, and by subdominant minor colouring at its second appearance in bars nineteen and twenty. A further effect arising out of this free exchange of tones and semitones is that tonic tonality is retained throughout the greater part of the answer's course.

Ex. 171 from Pachelbel provides an exact parallel:

Ex. 171. PACHELBEL, ORGAN FUGUE IN C

The answer in the final fugal section of Handel's *Dixit Dominus* provides a fascinating study in several respects:

Ex. 172A. Handel, Dixit Dominus

As will be seen, the answer replies tonally to the subject's initial dominant, but instead of completing itself thereafter at the upper fifth as normally one would expect,[9] it readjusts after only two notes at this level to subdominant level of *pitch*, at the same time adroitly avoiding subdominant *tonality*. In consequence, the tone-semitone sequence of the subject (as indeed in Ex. 119) becomes frequently reversed in the answer.

There would appear to be no immediately apparent reason for this unusual form of answer, other than that of replying tonally to the subject's second dominant in bar three. Even so, continuation at subdominant level following this point is not strictly necessary, as the melodic structure permits a further readjustment to dominant level:

Ex. 172B.

Which is how Frescobaldi resolves a closely similar situation:[10]

Ex. 173. FRESCOBALDI, CANZONA

Added together the expedients in *Dixit Dominus* result in the tonality confining itself almost exclusively to the tonic and its related key (B flat major) to a point well beyond the exposition. The dominant key is not even hinted at.

It should be obvious that underlying all this is some deeper significance, and it is my own belief that Handel's unusual answer has its explanation in the overall tonal design, not only of the final chorus, but of the work as a whole. The final chorus, which culminates in a five-part fugue, is 175 bars long. Throughout this vast movement, the home tonic (G minor) is seldom lost sight of. The fugal section accounts for the main part of the movement (121 bars), and we have to wait until the fugue has run almost half its course before the key of the dominant is touched upon. Its ultimate appearance, although brief, is a telling one, as it marks the physical climax of this great movement. From that point on, it is again the home tonic that predominates. Thus, the purpose of Handel's unusual answer becomes plain—a deliberate staving off of dominant tonality.

Furthermore, viewed against the conception of the work's grand overall tonal design, we see the final chorus as balancing the first part of the work; the two outer pillars of a broad ternary pattern, with the central episode of the work (No. 6) keeping mainly to the key of the dominant and its relative major.

Examined in isolation, apart from the body of the work itself, Handel's answer would appear perverse, and more than a little difficult to understand; but viewed in proper perspective, the part in relation to the whole, these apparent difficulties disappear.

Incidentally, both this answer and that in Ex. 173 further upset the 'notes of the tonic chord' theory.

In all these examples, the subtle tonal interplay between subject and answer is a value

---

[9]   See p. 86, (iii).
[10] Even so, in a subsequent entry of the answer, Frescobaldi follows the more usual procedure of replying to the subject's initial D tonally, and the remainder at the upper fifth.

that must be sacrificed if exactness of reply be insisted upon. Most would agree that a momentary relaxation is but a small price to pay for an outcome so delightfully refreshing as Ex. 171 on pp. 177–8 from Pachelbel. To heed the cautionary note of theory is to restrict tonal freedom. Independence, on the other hand, is sometimes achieved only by allowing oneself the very 'freedoms' that Prout for example prohibits. Yet he himself came very near the truth of the matter, for in singling out the fourth and seventh degrees ('this is especially the case with the subdominant and leading note'), he is to be seen trembling on the brink. Had he paused to reflect a little longer, he might have seen that a 'flattened' leading note can be instrumental in deferring modulation (as in Exx. 168, pp. 173–5 and 170, pp. 176–7), and a 'raised' subdominant (as in Ex. 174), in bringing it about.

Ex. 174.   J. S. Bach, Organ Prelude and Fugue in C

2. SUSPENSIONS

Kitson writes:

It is always better to let what in the Subject is a suspended discord remain so in the Answer. Bach, in *The Art of Fugue* . . .[11] gives the following:

Ex. 175A.   J. S. Bach, The Art of Fugue, Contrapunctus X

It is difficult to understand why he did not write:

Ex. 175B.

Similarly he answers:

Ex. 176A.   J. S. Bach, Organ Prelude and Fugue in C

by

[11] *Contrapunctus* X, bar 23.

Ex. 176B.   IBID.

Whereas one would have expected:[12]

Ex. 176c.

The only inference to be drawn from Kitson's criticism is that he could not have examined either work sufficiently, for out of the seven harmonized entries of the subject in Contrapunctus X, never once does Bach treat the tied quaver as a suspended discord, but as part of essential harmony. (See bars 26, 34, 47, 69, 78, 106, and 118.) Indeed, had Kitson examined *The Art of Fugue* more closely, he would have discovered that Bach treats the tied quaver as a harmony note in all eight entries of the theme in this particular form in Contrapunctus III, in all six entries in Contrapunctus IV, and in seven out of eight entries in Contrapunctus V. Similarly, in the C major Organ Fugue, Ex. 176a, it is only in three of some eleven entries of the subject in this form that Bach treats the tied note as a suspension. In the remaining entries it is part of essential harmony.[13] That Bach treats the tied note in the subject as a suspension on some occasions and not on others provides ample justification, surely, for similar freedom in the answer.

These considerations apart, there are two very good reasons against Kitson's alternative answer. The first is that Bach's own solution succeeds in retaining the main melodic characteristics of the subject (compare the melodic outlines of subject and answer in Ex. 177a with that in Ex. 177b); and the second, that against Bach's free tonal design, subject and answer must now result in a symmetrical alternation between tonic and dominant.[15]

Ex. 177A.

Ex. 177B.

Ex. 176a is also included in Ex. 126, of which group I have said that experiment will prove how very difficult it is to effect mutation satisfactorily at any point other than that chosen by the composers (p. 126). Kitson's experiment is a case in point.

---

[12] *Fugal Construction*, p. 25.
[13] Kitson make an equally curious error, when of the G minor Organ Fugue (Ex. 104a, p. 99) he writes: 'It will be observed that Bach does not attempt to present the following Subject in the major key', [14] for there are middle entries in B flat, F, and E flat majors.
[14] *Fugal Construction*, p. 13.
[15] See pp. 133–4, Section 3.

CHAPTER VIII

CHROMATIC SUBJECTS

Certain difficulties arise when it comes to finding an answer to a chromatic subject of the type which invites tonal reply. These difficulties stem from the consequences of tonal answer, whereby the interval of a fifth must contract into a fourth, and that of a fourth expand into a fifth. Not a few theorists take the view that real answers should be given to such subjects in order to preserve their special character. Richter for example concedes, 'we have no resource but to break the first rule of fugue-writing',[1] and both Higgs[2] and Prout[3] state simply, that chromatic subjects generally have real answers. However, beginning, I believe, with Fétis, successive French theorists including H. R. Colet, Gédalge, and Koechlin have given detailed instructions for finding *tonal* answers to subjects which ascend or descend chromatically between tonic and dominant, or between mediant and dominant. Exx. 37a–c, and 38a on p. 36 (whose answers were roundly condemned by Tovey—pp. 36–37) provide instances of this. Of Ex. 37a–c Gédalge writes: 'The first degree of the principle key occupies in the scale of the dominant the same interval as the fourth degree of the key of the dominant; consequently, in the answer, the fourth degree must be repeated until it actually does imitate the fourth degree of the principal key.'[4] Gédalge later renews discussion on this point, when he adds the following examples:[5]

EX. 178A.　GÉDALGE, TRAITÉ DE LA FUGUE

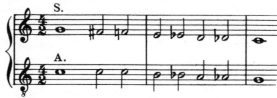

EX. 178B.　IBID.

Exx. 37 and 178 are used by Gédalge to illustrate the further point he makes, that it is not permitted for the answer to imitate the subject by contrary motion;[6] thus the answer in Ex. 178a could not take the form, C– C sharp – C – B – B flat etc., because the upward move C – C sharp is in contrary motion to the corresponding point in the subject. Koe-

---

[1] *Canon and Fugue*, p. 51.
[2] *Fugue*, p. 26.
[3] *Fugue*, p.64.
[4] *Traité*, pp. 22–23, para. 47.
[5] pp. 50–55, paras. 92–98.
[6] p. 22, para. 46.

chlin[7] and Dent[8] quote this same rule. Even so, it is clear that Gédalge regards the answers in Exx. 37 and 178 as hypothetical cases, for after commenting upon the consequent distortion of the subject's original shape, he concedes that subjects of this type are usually given *real* answers! Koechlin on the other hand upholds the *tonal* answer in such cases as the traditional method of reply, and later sets out to practise what he has preached by writing five expositions 'on a difficult Subject by Gédalge', giving a tonal answer in each case.[9]

Gédalge's rules and musical examples, like those of H. R. Colet before him,[10] are virtually the same as those given by Fétis;[11] even Gédalge's final concession in coming down on the side of real answer is hardly original, for Fétis, in his summing up, admits that a real answer, after all, is the only satisfactory way of replying to a chromatic subject!

The evidence of practice makes it clear that there is no one particular method of response. The group of musical examples which follows illustrates various forms of answer to subjects of this type.

(i) *Ascending, commencing on tonic.*

Ex. 179. PACHELBEL, INTERLUDES TO THE MAGNIFICAT, VII. 7

(ii) *Descending, commencing on tonic.*

Ex. 180A. J. S. BACH, CLAVIER TOCCATA IN F SHARP MINOR

Ex. 180B. PACHELBEL, ORGAN FUGUE IN D MINOR

Ex. 180C. GOTTLIEB MUFFAT, CLAVIER AND ORGAN FUGUE IN E MINOR

For a further real answer in this category, see J. S. Bach, Organ Fugue in E minor, BWV 548.

[7] *Etude*, p. 7 (fn 1).
[8] See p. 37.
[9] *Etude*, pp. 136–8.
[10] *La panharmonie musicale*, p. 237.
[11] *Traité*, p. 41.

For further tonal answers, see particularly Ex. 145 (p. 156), and Exx. 146–7 (pp. 156–7). It will be recalled that Mozart's answer (Ex. 145) was adversely criticized by Prout, who suggested a real answer in its place. (See p. 156.)

(iii) *Ascending, commencing on dominant.*

Ex. 181A.   PACHELBEL, INTERLUDES TO THE MAGNIFICAT, I. 19

Ex. 181B.   GOTTLIEB MUFFAT, CLAVIER AND ORGAN FUGUE IN C MINOR

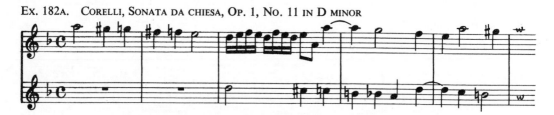

See also Ex. 116, p. 105 (*Chromatic Fantasia and Fugue*), and the comment on Ex.101c, pp. 95–6.

(iv) *Descending, commencing on dominant.*

Ex. 182A.   CORELLI, SONATA DA CHIESA, OP. 1, NO. 11 IN D MINOR

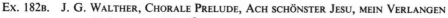

Ex. 182B.   J. G. WALTHER, CHORALE PRELUDE, ACH SCHÖNSTER JESU, MEIN VERLANGEN

Ex. 182C.   GOTTLIEB MUFFAT, CLAVIER AND ORGAN FUGUE IN A MINOR

Ex. 182D.   J. S. BACH, CLAVIER FUGUE IN E MINOR

The subdominant answer yields a double advantage; dominant is replied to by tonic, and the chromatic scale-line preserved intact. Ex. 39 on p. 37 from Thomas Attwood's *Kompositionsstudien* also fits into this category. Incidentally this was the only example encountered of an answer bearing resemblance to the type devised by the French theorists. Could it be coincidence that the only other answer found approximating to this same shape (because of its thrice sounded D) came from Attwood's teacher, Mozart? (Ex. 145, p. 156.)

(v) *Cases other than above.*

Ex. 183. Frescobaldi, Recercar Cromaticho

To summarize: although categories (i) and (ii) include examples of the dominant being replied to by tonic (tonal) on some occasions, and supertonic (real) on others, it is significant that in the three remaining categories (whose subjects, with one exception, commence on the dominant) this note consistently is replied to by tonic. It lends support first, to the claim made in Chapter IV, that in both the Renaissance and the Baroque a subject's initial dominant almost invariably is replied to by tonic; and second, to the theories advanced in Chapter V relating to subdominant and partial subdominant answers. (See Ex. 182a–d.)

Finally, Exx. 179–183 demonstrate that neither the tonal nor the real answer is recognized in practice as the normal method of reply to a chromatic subject.

CONCLUSION

A discussion of the theorists' arbitrary distinction between so-called 'students' ' (academic) and 'composers' ' (living) fugue is beyond the scope of this work. Those interested in this question may care to read Chapter V, 'Textbook Versus History', of Alfred Mann's *The Study of Fugue* for a penetrating treatment of the issue. But whatever the merits or demerits of the system, it is open to dispute whether the answer is an aspect of fugue that can be dealt with in a wholly satisfactory manner by the textbook, because the reasons for its form vary from one case to the next. Thus we cannot generalize.

First let the principle be accepted that a subject inviting a tonal response is normally given one. After that, reasons accounting for any deviation from this norm can be discovered only by subjecting each case to individual examination. Several varying factors such as melodic shape (although here one should learn to tread warily), limitations of a period's harmonic technique, tonality, and overall formal design, have already been advanced as possible influences on an answer's form; and although these appear to be the main factors, this is not to say that they are the only ones. Why for example, after an unbroken succession of *tonal* answers in the relevant exposition sections of Contrapunctus I–X in *The Art of Fugue*, does Bach for no immediately apparent reason decide upon a *real* answer to the opening subject of Contrapunctus XI?

A. W. Marchant's theory 'a real answer is here given, probably in order to preserve the melodic character of subject in the answer'[1] is weakened by this particular answer's very isolation in this respect, for no other *Art of Fugue* subject approximating to this particular shape is answered *other* than tonally. It would appear to me to stem from one of two interlinked reasons; either from a desire to avoid a subdominant answer (which a tonal reply would produce), or from the incidence of the physical link between Contrapunctus XI as a whole, and Contrapunctus VIII, whose three subjects are reworked in inversion.

Apart from some mutual exchanges of tone and semitone relationships, it will be seen that the subject which opens Contrapunctus XI is an exact inversion at the twelfth of the complementary subject in Contrapunctus VIII: (bars ninety-four et. seq.).

Ex. 184A.   J. S. BACH, THE ART OF FUGUE, CONTRAPUNCTUS VIII

---

[1] *Fugue Subjects*, p. 94, Ex. 492a.

Ex. 184B.   IBID., CONTRAPUNCTUS XI

It will further be seen that an exact inversion in Contrapunctus XI of the tonal answer of VIII would unavoidably result in a subdominant reply from its second note onwards, against the *dominant* reply of the earlier Contrapunctus. Also, whereas in, say, Contrapunctus X, and *Inversus* of the 'mirror' fugue of Contrapunctus XVI the melodic formation of their respective answers lends itself to tonal manipulation (a return from the sub-dominant to the tonic key being effected in both cases), that of XI precludes this.

In the case under discussion one cannot expect to have it both ways; if it is to be a tonal answer, then as a consequence one must be prepared to accept a disturbed melodic-harmonic relationship between the original and its inversion—the inversion at the twelfth shrinking at this point to one at the eleventh, resulting in turn in a subdominant answer. If, on the other hand, melodic-harmonic relationships between subject and answer are to be preserved, then one must be prepared to accept a real reply.

One of two possible ways out is to repeat the D in the answer's first bar as in Contrapunctus XIX, Ex. 35c (p. 35). The other is to give a tonal reply (letting the answer run on at subdominant level of *pitch*), but manoeuvring the tonality into the dominant *key*, by writing according to the A minor melodic scale. Like Handel in Ex. 119 (p. 107) you will gain your point (which is avoidance of subdominant tonality), but at the cost of reversing almost entirely the interval relationships between subject and answer.

Neither alternative is likely to commend itself. Indeed, experiment as you may, you will discover that Bach's answer is the most satisfactory way out.

Thus for each individual deviation from the 'rule'.

Throughout this work I have endeavoured to show the futility of attempting to devise a set of rules for fugal answer. To attempt to generalize could land one in no less sticky a morass. For example, what manner of rule could possibly be devised to meet the case, say, of the subject whose line has more than one appearance of the dominant note—

and there are numerous examples of this. Prout answers this emphatically: 'The rule of answering tonic by dominant, and dominant by tonic, *applies only to the beginning of a subject and to passages where a modulation to the dominant occurs*. . . . There is no mistake which students are more apt to make in beginning to write tonal answers than to answer dominant by tonic every time these notes occur. This is almost invariably wrong.'[2]

Although it is conceded that this is so in the majority of cases,[3] a rule such as this leaves one still guessing, as it fails to offer positive guidance. The theorist's dilemma is aggravated by such uncomfortable exceptions as Ex. 172a on p. 178. It takes but one exception to render any rule on the subject quite useless. It would be absurd to suggest that Handel is here breaking a rule. Neither can it be upheld as an 'exception to the rule', as similar 'exceptions' may be seen, for instance, in Ex. 99d (p. 88) and 99r (p. 90). The composers are simply answering their own subjects in their own manner.

Because fugue is as much a free expression of a composer's original ideas as any other musical form, I have attempted to prove by numerous examples from living music that criticism of an answer's melodic shape can only be subjective, unless of course, one is prepared to run the almost certain risk of seeing one's criticism rebound.

The answer differs from certain other aspects of fugue, such as inversion, invertible counterpoint, and the construction of episodes in that there is no need to be a skilled contrapuntist in order to find a musically satisfying (rather than 'correct') answer to a fugue subject. Right from the start the student should be made aware of the fact that the finding of a musicianly answer to a fugue subject depends in the first place upon detailed observation of past practice, and then upon applied musical judgement.

Until fugal answer ceases to be explained from the standpoint of the hard-and-fast rule, individual judgement must continue to be stifled, and a true appreciation of the very period which after all gave us the fugue, unnecessarily retarded.

---

[2] *Fugue*, p. 34, para. 88.
[3] See p. 86, (iii).

BIBLIOGRAPHY

ALBRECHTSBERGER, JOHANN GEORG. *Gründliche Anweisung zur Composition*, Leipzig, 1790. Trans. by A. Merrick, 2 vols., 2nd ed., London, 1844.

ARNOLD, F. T. *The Art of Accompaniment from a Thorough-Bass*, London, 1931.

ATTWOOD, THOMAS. *Theorie- und Kompositionsstudien bei Mozart*. (*Wolfgang Amadeus Mozart, Neue Ausgabe sämtlicher Werke*, Kassel, 1965, X/30/1.)

BACH, CARL PHILIPP EMANUEL. *Essay on the True Art of Playing Keyboard Instruments*, Berlin, 1753—1762. Trans. and ed. by William J. Mitchell, 2nd ed., London, 1951.

BAIRSTOW, EDWARD C. *Counterpoint and Harmony*, London, 1937.

BERNHARD, CHRISTOPH. *Tractatus compositionis augmentatus*, c. 1650. Ed. J. M. Müller-Blattau, Leipzig, 1926.

CAUS, SALOMON DE. *Institution harmonique*, Frankfurt, 1615.

The Musical Quarterly, XXXVI (1950); XXXVII (1951).

CHERUBINI, LUIGI. *A Treatise on Counterpoint and Fugue*. Eng. trans. by Cowden Clarke, London, 1854.

COCKSHOOT, JOHN V. *The Fugue in Beethoven's Piano Music*, London, 1959.

COLET, HIPPOLYTE RAYMOND. *La panharmonie musicale*, Paris, 1837.

DENT, E. J. *Notes on Fugue for Beginners*, Cambridge, 1958.

DICKINSON, A. E. F. *Bach's Fugal Works*, London, 1956.

DUNSTAN, RALPH. *A Cyclopaedic Dictionary of Music*, 4th ed., London, 1925.

FÉTIS, FRANCOIS JOSEPH. *Traité du contrepoint et de la fugue*, Paris, 1824. New edition, Paris, 1846.

FUX, JOHANN JOSEPH. *Gradus ad Parnassum*, Vienna, 1725. Section on *The Study of Counterpoint*, trans. and ed. Alfred Mann, London, 1944. Section on *The Study of the Fugue*, trans. and ed. Alfred Mann, *The Musical Quarterly*, XXXVI (1950), XXXVII (1951).

GÉDALGE, ANDRÉ. *Traité de la fugue*, Paris, 1901.

Grove's Dictionary of Music and Musicians, 3rd ed., London, 1929, II, article, *Harmony*; 5th ed., London, 1954, III, article *Fugue*.

HIGGS, JAMES. *Fugue*, London, 1878.

HOME, ETHEL. *Short History of Music*, London, 1926.

HORSLEY, IMOGENE. *Fugue— History and Practice*, New York, 1966.

HUDSON, FREDERICK. Hallische Händel-Ausgabe, Serie IV. Band 11, *Sechs Concerti Grossi Opus 3, Kritischer Bericht*, Kassel, 1963.

HUTCHINGS, ARTHUR. *The Invention and Composition of Music*, London, 1958.

JEPPESON, KNUD. *Counterpoint*, trans. Glen Haydon, London, 1950.

KELLER, GODFREY. *A Complete Method for Attaining to Play a Thorough-Bass upon either Organ, Harpsichord, or Theorbo Lute*, London, 1707.

KITSON, C. H. *The Elements of Fugal Construction*, London, 1929.

KOECHLIN, CHARLES. *Etude sur l'écriture de la fugue d'école*, Paris, 1933.

LANG, PAUL HENRY. *Music in Western Civilization*, New York, 1941.

LOVELOCK, WILLIAM. *The Examination Fugue*, London, n.d.

LOWINSKY, EDWARD E. *Tonality and Atonality in Sixteenth-Century Music*, Berkeley, 1961.

MACPHERSON, STEWART. *Studies in the Art of Counterpoint*, London, 1927.

MANN, ALFRED. *The Study of Fugue*, New Brunswick, N.J., 1958.

MARCHANT, ARTHUR W. *Five Hundred Fugue Subjects and Answers*, 2nd ed., London, 1892.

MARPURG, FRIEDRICH WILHELM. *Abhandlung von der Fuge*, 2nd ed., Leipzig, 1806.

MATTHESON, JOHANN. *Der vollkommene Capellmeister*, Hamburg, 1739.

MORLEY, THOMAS. *A Plaine and Easie Introduction to Practicall Musicke*, 1597. New ed. by R. Alec Harman, London, 1952.

MORRIS, R. O. *The Structure of Music*, London, 1935.

NIVERS, GUILLAUME GABRIEL. *Traité de la composition de musique*, Paris, 1667.

OLDROYD, GEORGE. *The Technique and Spirit of Fugue*, London, 1948.

PLAYFORD, JOHN. *An Introduction to the Art of Descant*, with additions by Henry Purcell, London, 1697.

PROUT, EBENEZER. *Fugue*, London, 1891.

PROUT, EBENEZER. *Harmony: Its Theory and Practice*, 16th ed., London, 1901.

RAMEAU, JEAN PHILIPPE. *Traité de l'harmonie*, Paris, 1722. Eng. edition, London, c. 1775.

RAMOS DE PAREJA, BARTOLOMÉ. *Musica practica*, 1482. Ed. Johannes Wolf (Internationalen Musikgesellschaft, *Beiheft* II), Leipzig, 1901.

REESE, GUSTAV. *Music in the Renaissance*, New York, 1959.

RICHTER, ERNST FRIEDRICH. *Lehrbuch der Fuge*, Leipzig, 1859. Eng. trans. Franklin Taylor, London, 1878.

SPITTA, PHILIPP. *Johann Sebastian Bach*, Leipzig, 1873–1880. Eng. trans. Clara Bell and J. A. Fuller—Maitland, New York, 1951.

STAINER AND BARRETT. *Dictionary of Musical Terms*, rev. and ed. J. Stainer, London, 1898.

TOVEY, DONALD FRANCIS. *A Musician Talks: 2. Musical Textures*, London, 1941.

TÜRK, DANIEL GOTTLOB. *Kurze Anweisung zum Generalbassspielen*, Halle and Leipzig, 1791.

VICENTINO, NICOLA. *L'antica Musica ridotta alla moderna prattica*, Rome, 1555.

ZARLINO, GIOSEFFO. *Istitutioni harmoniche*, Venice, ed. of 1589.

INDEX OF MUSICAL EXAMPLES

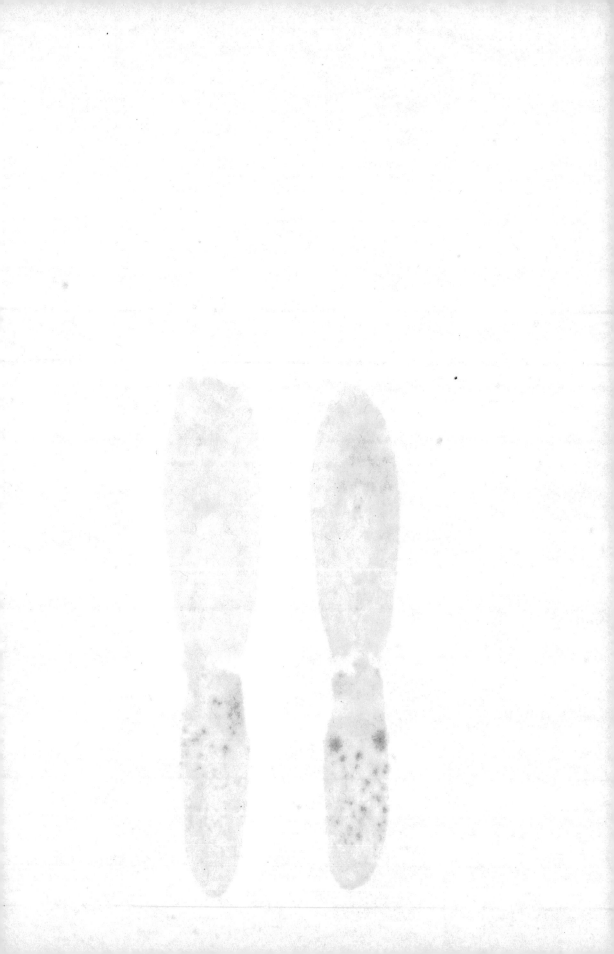

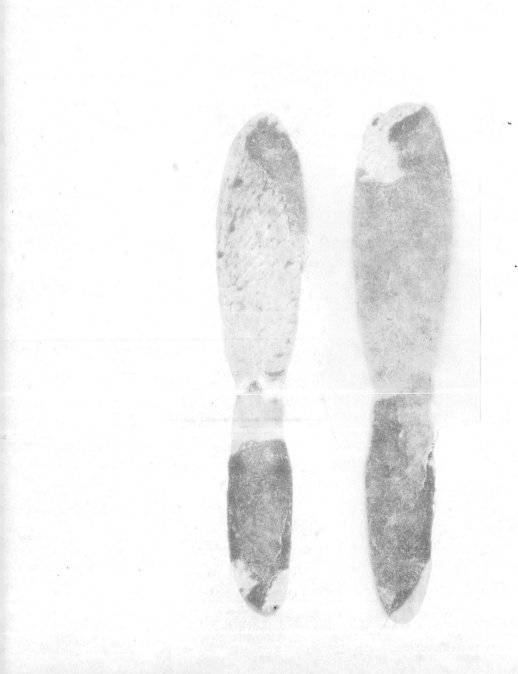